From her special perch outside the news director's office at the CBS-owned TV station in Los Angeles, Lorraine Hillman witnessed up close the birth and development of local television, and especially, local TV news. Joining the fabled KNXT "Big News" in 1963 as only the second woman in the newsroom, she served for almost four decades as the administrative gatekeeper to a long succession of news executives and as the "Mother Superior" to a legendary parade of famous and near-famous news personalities from Maury Povich to Connie Chung. And in the process, she found herself involved firsthand in the coverage of some of the nation's most compelling news stories, including the O. J. Simpson saga, and in the 1970s, the kidnapping of Patty Hearst and the SLA shootout. Her story is the story of broadcast news itself, coming of age in the socially tumultuous 1960s and persevering into the twenty-first century and the advent of social media.

—Bill Applegate

Lorraine Hillman was one of the pioneers in the early days of television news. She saw a great deal and tucked it away in her memory. For a history of Los Angeles television, few people would know the terrain better than Lorraine. For those of you who were around at that time, it will remind you of those heady days when television news actually featured news.

——Marcia Brandwynne

If anyone knows what the TV business was like before women were allowed, it's Lorraine Hillman. She is a remarkable woman with a remarkable talent who had a remarkable career. Television needs more talent like Lorraine Hillman.

——Dave Lopez, TV broadcast reporter for forty-five years in Los Angeles

It was the 1970s—a time when men dominated TV news, and women didn't help one another very often. Yet Lorraine, the secretary to the news director, listened sympathetically to me, a twenty-five-year-old, as I begged for the chance to break into journalism. She used her wiles to get me an interview, and that launched my thirty-two-year career as a reporter. Lorraine was a smart, kind, and influential figure behind the scenes in a world where women were frequently dismissed as inferior in intelligence and judgment. Like most women in those days, she worked for the men. But Lorraine always supported the women. She was one of the central players in the drama/comedy that would become the heyday of local news in LA.

—Linda Douglass

Lorraine was the heart, soul, and most importantly, the motor of KNXT-TV News (now KCBS). Forget about the men who held the titles of news director, a revolving door of suits. You must read her book. She knows and tells all.

—Connie Chung

Lifetime of News

Lifetime of News

A Memoir

To Dennis,
Wishing you a Lifetime
of News,
Best,
Loraine Hillman
March, 2018

Lorraine Hillman

ISBN-13: 9781544742168
ISBN-10: 1544742169
Library of Congress Control Number: 2017904308
CreateSpace Independent Publishing Platform
North Charleston, South Carolina

Cover photo courtesy CBS ALUMNI

FOR ROB

Contents

Foreword

*L*ifetime *of News*, a memoir of Lorraine Hillman's breakthrough career in broadcast news, is the fascinating story of how a young mother splintered the glass ceiling that denied employment to qualified women no matter how skilled they might be. The year was 1963 when the groundbreaking first-in-the-nation hour-long *Big News* on KNXT, the CBS-owned station in Los Angeles, was playing to record audiences led by its golden-haired anchorman, Jerry Dunphy. When Lorraine walked into the cigarette smoke-filled newsroom, there was a certain amount of trepidation in her gait. And who could blame her? The only other woman in the place was Bette Penny, the personal secretary of news director Roy Heatly and, previous to him, Sam Zelman, creator of *The Big News*. They were the only women employed in the hallowed CBS studio at Sunset and Gower. There were no other minorities, no blacks, and no Hispanics. But that would soon change, and Lorraine was in the vanguard of that change.

She was a skilled researcher and jack-of-all-trades, a single mother who, by sheer diligence, worked her way up to a cherished job at the network of Edward R. Murrow. Lorraine was a font of information on such major stories as the Manson murders, the assassination of

Senator Robert F. Kennedy, the O. J. Simpson double murder case and countless other Hollywood headline stories. As producer of *The Big News*, I valued her ability to dig up information that gave a distinctive edge to our news coverage. Today, there are more women than men gainfully employed in the business of broadcast news. Lorraine Hillman set the standard for all of them. Her story is one that must be read by anyone who wants to understand the nuances of broadcast journalism.

—Pete Noyes

Introduction

As a kid growing up in Hollywood, there was no TV, Internet, iPhones, e-mail, texting, or tweets. I was very small when my parents took me to horse races at Santa Anita, Del Mar, and Caliente in Tijuana, baseball at Pan Pacific, midget-auto racing, and gambling ships anchored three miles off the coast of California and reached by water taxi. I grew up listening to radio shows like *The Adventures of Sam Spade, Lux Radio Theatre*, and *The Jack Benny Program* and using my imagination while hearing dialogue and sound effects. Later, I read daily newspapers; Los Angeles had four. And I read movie magazines. I collected autographs from famous movie stars, among them teen-age Elizabeth Taylor, Ava Gardner, Ronald Reagan, Jane Wyman, Mickey Rooney, and Donald O'Connor. I developed an appetite for news through reading newspapers, and later, from watching television coverage. I decided I wanted to work in a newsroom, but getting hired was a long time coming.

My effort to pursue that goal started in 1957, when CBS Television hired me as an entry-level secretary at Television City. Six years later, when I moved to CBS/KNXT, Channel 2 News, I became the news director's right hand, working on major news stories such as Manson, McMartin, Menendez, Hillside Strangler, The Night Stalker, Patty Hearst and the SLA shootout, Michael Jackson, the *Twilight Zone* accident, earthquakes, fires, floods, the O. J. Simpson criminal and civil trials. I retired from Channel 2 News and returned to work, this time at ABC News's Los Angeles Bureau. With a career in news spanning forty years, I worked under news directors Roy Heatly, Grant Holcomb, Bill Eames, Jim Topping, Sam Zelman (creator of *The Big News* in the early 1960s, he returned as a consultant news director), Bob Schaefer, Jay Feldman, Johnathan Rodgers, and Steve Cohen. Following my promotion to director of news research and executive producer of *Newsmakers*, I reported to news directors Andy Fisher (acting news director Don Dunkel), Eric Sorenson, Michael Singer, Jose Rios, John Lippman, Bob Jordan, and Larry Perrett.

The general managers I worked for from 1963 to 1995 were Bob Wood, Ray Beindorf, Bill O'Donnell, Russ Barry, Chris Desmond, Van Gordon Sauter, Ed Joyce, Jamie Bennett, Frank Gardner, Tom van Amburg, Bob Hyland, Steve Gigliotti, and Bill Applegate.

This book is indeed a lifetime of news.

Chapter 1

Growing Up in LA

I was born Lorraine Pauline Post in Los Angeles, California. My birth took place at LA County Hospital during the Great Depression. My father worked as a carpenter. He joined crews building homes in locations such as Toluca Lake, where he worked on construction of Bing Crosby's home, as well as other stars'residences. I attended kindergarten and first grade at Lockwood Elementary School in Hollywood. My mother and father separated when I was seven. We lived on Melrose Avenue, near Vermont. When my parents separated, I was sent to live with my grandparents on my mother's side in Burbank and attended Saint Robert Bellermine Elementary School.

I don't have a lot of childhood memories, but one that stands out is from December 7, 1941. My parents and I had spent the day at Caliente Race Track in Tijuana. We headed home, and I was sitting in the rumble seat of my father's car. When we reached the Mexico/California border, there was a commotion, with lots of people in the streets, and we didn't understand what was happening. It wasn't until after we crossed the border into the United States that we learned the Japanese had bombed Pearl Harbor. We listened over the radio to President Roosevelt describe the bombing as a "day of infamy."

The United States went to war, and rationing was introduced. I remember going to the local movies, which cost a quarter—and that included a candy bar. The theater held a drawing for a pound of margarine. That was a big prize, because butter was rationed, along with several other food items, during the war. The margarine was the kind that came with a little packet of coloring powder so that it could be turned from white to yellow and made to look like butter. I was the proud winner of the prize.

I lived in many different places as a child, and because of the moves, was never in a particular school long enough to make friends, save my best friend, Marie, whom I met in junior high. I attended Lockwood Elementary in LA, Saint Robert Bellermine in Burbank, Immaculate Heart of Mary Elementary School on Santa Monica Boulevard in Hollywood, Lockwood again, Thomas Starr King Junior High in Los Feliz, John Muir Junior High in southwest LA, and Manual Arts High School.

At Immaculate Heart of Mary, I sat next to a kid named Dwayne Hickman. We were members of Sister Stanislaus's fifth-grade class. She was the cruelest nun, and I thought I was the only target of her mean streak, but at the time, I was very young. Dwayne and I both ended up at CBS Television, he after a successful run as the star of the popular television show *The Many Loves of Dobie Gillis* and later as a television network executive. When I spoke to him about our time at Immaculate Heart, it turned out his memory of Sister Stanislaus was the same as mine. Somehow, I felt better knowing I wasn't the only one who incurred her wrath.

When I was a student at John Muir Junior High School, I was called in to meet with a woman guidance counselor to discuss my future career path. I knew what I wanted that path to be. Because

I was attending *Sam Spade* radio broadcast recordings every week at CBS Columbia Square in Hollywood, I wanted to go into radio acting. I wanted to be like actress Lurene Tuttle, who was a regular with Howard Duff on the *Sam Spade* program; Lurene played his secretary, Effie. My goal was to take drama classes. The guidance counselor dismissed my idea and said, "Oh no, that's not a profession you should be thinking about. Girls have two paths…girls can be nurses or teachers."

Chapter 2

Family History

My grandparents on my father's side were devout practicing members of the Free Methodist Church; my grandfather Post was a retired Free Methodist minister. My father was the black sheep of the family. He married my mother in a Catholic ceremony, and I was baptized and raised in the Catholic faith. My father, Lewis Dixon Post, was born in Niles, Michigan, and moved with his family when he was young to Highland Park, a suburb of Los Angeles.

The Post side of my family had an interesting ancestral history. Although we are no relation to the Post Cereal family or to Emily Post, our Posts did have a famous ancestor: Sir Joseph Lister (April 5, 1827 to February 10, 1912), the father of modern antiseptic surgery. A British surgeon and scientist who promoted the idea of sterile surgery and for whom Listerine was named, Lister was raised to the peerage in 1897, and the title of Baron Lister was bestowed.

When doctors ask about my family health history, their interest is piqued. My father and his three brothers died young as the result of heart attacks; however, his three sisters lived to old age, into their nineties. My grandfather, my dad, and his three brothers all suffered from a form of palsy. It wasn't Parkinson's disease but exhibited the same symptoms—shaking of the hands and head. Again, his three sisters never showed any symptoms. A neurologist once told me there are several non-Parkinson's diseases, such as essential tremors, that display symptoms similar to Parkinson's. Actress Katharine Hepburn, for instance, spoke in interviews about her palsy-type symptoms and said people thought she had Parkinson's when, in fact, she didn't. Since my father never saw a doctor, he was never officially diagnosed. The following generation of males did not exhibit symptoms of the affliction.

My maternal grandfather, William McMahon, was a newspaperman, and when a job became available on the West Coast, he and his wife, Alice, relocated from New York to Burbank, California. My grandmother Alice lived to be 102. She entered a nursing home in her late nineties and had all her faculties until the day she died. Once I received a phone message at work from the nursing home administrator to tell me that my grandmother went to a pay phone and called a taxi cab to pick her up, asking the driver to bring her home to her house in Culver City. Luckily, he checked with the nursing staff, and her nickname became Alibi Alice. On the occasion of Alice's one-hundredth birthday, our family threw her a big birthday party. My son, Rob, read a special message to her—a framed birthday greeting in honor of this milestone from Nancy and President Ronald Reagan.

Alice was the youngest of nine. Her sister Nell lived in Los Angeles, and I got to know her; we became close when I was growing up. Nell was taller than my grandmother. When she walked into a room, you felt her presence. She had been married three times, first to a bigamist, the second she didn't talk about, and third to her husband, Karl, who passed away many years before Aunt Nell. Her hair was snow white. She was always dressed to the hilt and wore expensive earrings and brooches. Nell was outgoing and vivacious. She was progressive and believed in furthering one's education no matter what age. She encouraged me to go back to school, even though it meant working all day and attending adult education classes at night. I admired her smarts, as she spoke with extraordinary knowledge about many subjects.

Aunt Nell was in her nineties when she confided in me that she was secretly working for the FBI in Los Angeles and had been attending so-called book club meetings and reporting back to an FBI agent about what transpired at the meetings. This was at a time when the McCarthy hearings were taking place before Congress, and certain Hollywood actors and writers were boycotted for allegedly having Communist Party leanings.

Chapter 3

Weekends at Columbia Square

Living in Hollywood as a child, kids collected autographs for entertainment. We gathered outside movie premieres, nightclubs such as Ciro's and Mocambo, radio shows such as *Lux Radio Theatre* on Vine Street, and at Columbia Square located at Sunset Boulevard and Gower. Kids waited outside the Columbia Square artists' entrance at the rear of the building just adjacent to the parking lot.

I met my best friend, Marie, also an autograph collector, at Thomas Starr King Junior High (now known as the middle school). We were both fans of actor Howard Duff and his *Sam Spade* radio show on CBS, so we joined the Howard Duff fan club. Along with actress Lurene Tuttle and a revolving cast of guest stars, he taped the *Sam Spade* program on Sundays in the early afternoon, and it aired nationally on Sunday nights. During the time the *Sam Spade* show was at Columbia Square, Jack Webb was doing radio, and Ira Grossel (later known as actor Jeff Chandler) was starring on a show called *Doctor Dana*. Both would occasionally guest on Duff's program, along with June Havoc (at that time married to the program's director, Bill Spear).

Marie and I, along with ten other youthful members of Duff's fan club, attended every recording. Howard Duff arrived at the studio, went inside briefly, then reappeared with tickets for us—tickets to the CBS sponsors' booth, which was located upstairs above the radio studio and had twelve seats and a large glass window where we could look down, watch the actors rehearse, and listen to the actual radio broadcast recording. He cared deeply about his fans, and we loved him for it. Duff also came out to the parking lot after the show and gave one of us his scripts, autographed to the lucky fan that week. He kept track, too, because if someone tried to put one over, he would say, "No, I gave *you* a script last week. Wait your turn."

Moving from Hollywood to southwest LA didn't stop me from Sundays at Columbia Square. I rode the yellow streetcar to Melrose and Vermont, near City College, where my friend's parents would pick me up, and they would drop us off to see the Duff show. One of the people who would be standing outside waiting for Duff was Tony Curtis (then Bernard Schwartz); he and Duff shared the same agent, Mike Meshikoff. Duff was dating actress Ava Gardner at the time, and he, Ava, and Tony would walk over to the Naples, an upscale bar/restaurant on Gower. Of course, we kids would tag behind, and watch them enter, but we weren't old enough to actually go to the Naples. Imagine my amazement many years later when I transferred to Columbia Square from Television City and could not only walk through the artists' entrance door without a ticket but also go up the stairs and enter the Naples! Years later, when Actor Tony Curtis came to Channel 2 News, Columbia Square, to be interviewed by our entertainment reporter, instead of sitting in the green room, he came down the hall to my research office after getting makeup, pulled up a chair, and we reminisced, sharing stories about those earlier times with Howard Duff, kids like myself, and radio show days.

My weekends at Columbia Square were a great experience. I have a treasured autograph book and happy memories of those days. It wasn't until *Sam Spade* moved to NBC at Sunset and Vine that the twelve of us fans could no longer attend. Howard Duff apologized for the slight on NBC's part; they didn't have a sponsors' booth or audience accommodation.

Columbia Square, photo courtesy of CBS Alumni

L to R, cousin Sharon Ronnie, myself and best friend Marie Gaines

Chapter 4

Developing a Passion through Early LA News

My interest in news developed early. We read daily newspapers or listened to radio for news—there was no social media, no YouTube, no Google, no Twitter. Later, when we became owners of a black-and-white television, we watched news interview programs featuring popular local LA news personalities Paul Coates and Tom Duggan. The two were the Sean Hannity and Bill O'Reilly of their day. Coates and Duggan were wildly popular for some indepth pieces but mainly for their delivery. Paul Coates, a former *LA Mirror* newspaper columnist, presented investigative stories in a series called *Confidential File*. Tom Duggan had a brash, controversial delivery style. He also had a bad habit of not showing up. Last-minute anchor substitutes were often called upon to replace him. On one of those occasions, a very young Regis Philbin subbed and, although nervous and frightened, he made such a good impression he went on to a job anchoring in San Diego.

Local news anchor George Putnam was immensely popular and owned the early LA television market for many years. Everyone watched Putnam. He was Mr. Popularity until he lost his objectivity and began an ongoing fight with Mayor Norris Poulson. He used his anchor platform each night to air his personal views about the LA mayor rather than delivering the day's news. George Putnam went from anchoring at KTTV to a stint at KTLA then back to KTTV and was the most familiar face and voice of Los Angeles television news until *The Big News* and anchor Jerry Dunphy arrived in 1961.

Three local news stories made lasting impressions on me. First was the 1947 murder of Elizabeth Short, nicknamed the Black Dahlia by the news media. Los Angeles and national newspapers covered every detail of the gruesome scene in the Leimert Park area extensively. Her murder remains unsolved to this day.

Second, Kathy Fiscus was a three-year-old girl who fell into an uncapped well in San Marino on April 8, 1949. A landmark television event, KTLA carried live, on-site coverage of the rescue attempt, with twenty-seven hours of continuous broadcast by reporter Stan Chambers, a man whom I later knew and was proud to have as a colleague in the news business for several years.

But the story that affected me most as a kid was the kidnapping and murder of six-year-old Linda Glucoft. (I was a latchkey kid before the term came into popular use. I lived with my mother but was alone a lot while she was away working. Before the Stroble case, I hadn't heard much about kidnapping.) The Glucoft family lived on Crescent Heights Boulevard, north of Culver City. Linda's playmate Rochelle lived across the street with her parents and grandfather, Fred Stroble, an unemployed baker. Sixty-seven-year-old Stroble had a record of exposing himself to children and an accusation of molestation. He had missed court appearances and had slipped through the judicial cracks. When Linda arrived at her friend's home on November 15, 1949, Stroble was the only one home, since Rochelle and her mother had gone to a birthday party. Linda's body was found the next day; she had been beaten, stabbed, and strangled.

Stroble fled but was captured three days later. He admitted to killing Linda to silence her screaming. The public was outraged that a sex offender was in the neighborhood, free to molest and murder. The Glucoft case resulted in California Governor Earl Warren enacting tougher laws and penalties for crimes against children. Fred Stroble was tried and convicted and was executed in San Quentin on Friday, July 25, 1952. The coverage of the Glucoft murder was something I never forgot.

Chapter 5

Domestic Violence: Warning Signs

During summer vacation from high school, I saw a job ad for a downtown theater usher. I took the streetcar at Forty-Eighth and Budlong to downtown LA. The line of applicants wound around the block on Sixth and Broadway. I didn't get that job, but the Forum Cafeteria down the street was hiring. They never asked my age, and so I found myself working full time on the cafeteria serving counter. I was quickly promoted to an office position, handling payroll and phones. When it came time to return to school in September, I decided to quit school and continue working.

I met my husband at the Forum. After a year of dating, with several breakups and makeups, we married, and I became a victim of domestic violence at age seventeen. I dated my husband, nine years my senior, for a year. There were signs of abuse during that year, but I thought I could change him, that what he needed was me. But after we married, the abuse, both verbal and physical, accelerated. He drank on the job and after work. When he was sober, he could be the sweetest man, but his personality changed when he was drinking. The abuse began with shoving, with no provocation. The shoving escalated into slapping and then hitting, punching, and kicking.

Then there was the burning with cigarettes. I would leave to go live with my grandmother and mother, but he would come after me, and his apologies would convince me to return to our home. A week, or maybe two, would go by, and the abuse would start again. He often was as nice as could be when he was sober, but when he drank, he turned into another man.

I was nineteen years old and pregnant when I left for good and moved in with my mother and grandmother; had I stayed, I may not have continued to full term. There was no option for a restraining order, and he threatened me. My son was born on June 20, 1953. It was the happiest day of my life. I found an attorney and got a divorce. I never regretted my marriage because I had a beautiful baby boy as a result. The best thing that ever happened to me was the birth of my son.

My ex-husband failed to provide financial support and threatened to kill me if I took him to court. At that time, Los Angeles County had a weak judicial system where the collection of support money was concerned. The only resource I had was the Failure to Provide Department of LA County, which was ineffective. The LA Superior Court judge I appeared before ordered my ex to pay twenty-five dollars a month in child support; he didn't comply. The Failure to Provide Department informed me they couldn't do anything to force him to pay until he had missed several months; he never paid, and they never pursued him. He proved to be an absentee father in every sense.

Nationally, there had been a long history of silence about domestic violence. There were no hotlines for battered women, no shelters, and no resources. Women didn't have rights of protection and few legal or financial means. Things began to change in the 1960s with the women's movement. Today, it's a lot different. There are government-supported legal resources and shelters for battered women.

Channel 2 News did many news stories about domestic abuse during my time there. Interviews with young women were always the same. They thought he would change. While dating, he would discourage her from seeing her friends or spending time with her family; he would cut her off from everyone but him. This treatment is a red flag. I decided to write about this part of my life in order to help other young women who might be in a similar situation while dating someone exhibiting abuse toward them. It doesn't get any better. It only gets worse. You cannot change him, and you shouldn't be blinded by love and your feelings for him. Painful as it might seem, it's best to break off the relationship.

If you find yourself in a situation of domestic abuse and need help, call the National Domestic Violence Hotline: 1-800-799-SAFE (7233).

Chapter 6

Making Ends Meet

When my son was three months old, I applied for a part-time job at the telephone company on Vernon Avenue, which was two blocks away, walking distance from where I lived on Harvard Boulevard. My grandmother cared for Rob while I worked four hours a day as an information operator. It was not an easy place to work in those days. To take a bathroom break, the operators raised their hands to seek permission from a supervisor. The supervisors explained that we operators weren't seen by the public, only heard, so there was no acceptable excuse for being absent for illness. When I came down with the flu, the doctor gave me penicillin, and I had an allergic reaction—itching, hives, and swelling over every part of my body. The reaction was so bad that I couldn't go to work. The doctor gave me some medicine in an attempt to counteract the symptoms, but it only worsened my condition. My supervisors at Pacific Telephone and Telegraph didn't believe I was ill; two of them came to my home to check and see for themselves.

While working as an operator, I found most people dialing for information were polite and appreciative. We were instructed not to be chatty with them; we were told to keep the calls moving, give the number they were seeking, and move on to the next call. However, there was a months-long period during my tenure when the company changed its policy. They decided to educate the public about using the telephone book and to teach them not to be dependent on Information as a source. My coworkers and I were sent to class to be educated in the future handling of callers seeking phone numbers. It seems laughable now. We were told to look up the number in our directories and then inform the caller, "That number is in *your* directory. Please look it up now." No caller was pleased with that response. I heard several excuses as to why they couldn't or wouldn't. I heard, "I'm blind," or "I can't reach the phone book," and the best one: "I'm sitting on the phone book." There were irate callers, cussing callers, and threatening callers.

I stayed with the phone company for about two years but eventually left to search for a full-time position elsewhere.

Chapter 7

MacGregor Sporting Goods: A Secretarial Start

I was taking a stenography course at Los Angeles Community College when a part-time job posting caught my eye at MacGregor's Sporting Goods, located at 14th and Flower Street The job was to take dictation and answer phones for the company's golf sales pro. MacGregor's didn't sell retail, only to golf pros and direct to retail sporting goods companies. I got the job and had been working part time about three months when the company's director, Bob DeVoe, approached me about working for him full time. I accepted. My son was two years old by then, I had no child support, and it was time for me to work full time. It had become too much for my grandmother to care for my son. I found a terrific woman named Jessie Carufo who provided child care in her home. She loved Rob, and he loved her.

At MacGregor's, I met athletes, golf pros, and sports agents and managers. Leo Durocher came in one day. When we were introduced, he said, "I'll have no trouble remembering your name, Lorraine," and he laughed. He was married to actress Laraine Day. Durocher had a colorful career, first as a baseball player and then as a manager for the

Me with my son Rob

Brooklyn Dodgers, New York Giants, Chicago Cubs, and Houston Astros. He was with the Brooklyn Dodgers from 1947 to 1956. In the spring of 1947, Durocher let it be known he would not tolerate team opposition to Jackie Robinson joining the club, saying, "I do not care if the guy is yellow or black, or if he has stripes like a fuckin' zebra. I'm the manager of this team, and I say he plays. What's more, I say he can make us all rich! And if any of you cannot use the money, I will see that you are traded." He called Robinson "a Durocher with talent." Later, after a stretch with the Giants, Durocher became a baseball commentator for NBC. In retirement, Durocher wrote a book with Ed Linn titled *Nice Guys Finish Last* and was elected posthumously to the Baseball Hall of Fame in 1994.

Chapter 8

Travels with Rob

As my son was growing up, I wanted him to see America's national parks. During my two-week vacations, we took road trips to Yosemite, Sequoia, and Redwoods National Parks and to Arizona's Grand Canyon. (Years later, when Rob had a job transfer to Tempe, Arizona, I visited his family, and he, in turn, took his kids and me to the Grand Canyon.)

Traveling with Rob

Rob was nine years old when we made a trip to Utah's Bryce Canyon and Zion National Park. In Bryce, we happened upon a film location. Production was under way on the set of *Sergeants 3* starring the Rat Pack, as they were known—friends and costars Frank Sinatra, Dean Martin, Sammy Davis Jr., Peter Lawford, and Joey Bishop. Another summer, we traveled to Grand Teton National Park, where we experienced outdoor barbecue and a show put on by Western riders and ropers.

I took my son, Rob, on a trip to Europe in June 1968 to meet my lifelong pen pal, Mary Carty, for the first time. When I was in elementary school, kids had the option of selecting an overseas pen pal from Britain or Ireland. Mary lived in Hebburn, County Durham, England. We exchanged handwritten letters and still write to this day, only now it's via e-mail. She married Bob Carty, and they adopted two daughters, Julie and Maria. They still reside in Hebburn.

We were scheduled for an organized coach trip of Europe, but prior to joining that tour, I planned a trip from London by train up to Newcastle, the closest city to Hebburn. The only problem was that, when Rob and I arrived in London, we discovered the trains were on a "go slow." The workers were on strike, and the trains simply were not scheduled to run. We couldn't get into a London hotel; they were booked because no one could get out of London due to the strike. I had the number for a producer at the BBC, given to me by one of our KNXT cameramen, Eli Ressler, who traveled extensively. He knew everyone and said to me, "Call this guy if you should need any help." It was Sunday. I phoned the BBC, and the person on duty listened to my plight and contacted that producer, and he called the phone booth I was waiting in while Rob sat patiently outside with our luggage. He said he and his wife would drive in to pick us up, and we would spend the night at their house in Surrey, a London suburb. I can never thank them enough for taking in total strangers.

The next morning, he drove us to Wimbledon, where he was producing the BBC coverage of the tennis matches. We waited at the Wimbledon train station and caught a "go-slow" train to Newcastle.

Mary and I had never met or seen photos of each other, and so we didn't know what to expect. She told me the following story after we'd been staying with her and Bob a few days. She and her husband were watching as the train arrived, and she saw a woman with a rather large picture hat and long cigarette holder step off the train, and she said to Bob, "My God, I hope that's not her." Mary said she breathed a sigh of relief when, seconds later, Rob and I stepped off the train. We found the people of Hebburn, Mary's neighbors, family, and everyone we passed in the street, to be open and welcoming to us Americans. Of course, Mary had told everyone her pen pal from the United States was visiting.

Rob and I next went to Belfast and took the train from Northern Ireland to the Republic of Ireland. The train conductor came down the aisle to check our passports and commented, "US, huh? Not carrying any guns, are ye?" It was two weeks after the assassination of Robert Kennedy in Los Angeles, and the remark stung. I had been working on the news election set the night Bobby Kennedy was shot at the Ambassador Hotel. We were about to go off the air when a call came from reporter Paul Udell at the Ambassador that Kennedy had been shot. It was another shock, following the assassination of his brother John in 1963 as well as Martin Luther King Jr.'s assassination on April 4, 1968, in Memphis, Tennessee.

I later made another trip to Hebburn, England, in 1997 with my grandson, Michael. The trip was his high school graduation gift. We planned to visit Mary, her husband, Bob, and their family. I thought Mike might become bored, since he was a teenager, and there might not be enough activity in Hebburn to interest him. I was wrong. Mary and Bob had a granddaughter, Carly, who was sixteen, the same age as Mike. A friendship, more like puppy love, developed. Mary asked me if I noticed that every time we entered a room, Carly and Mike left. When it came time to leave, both kids were teary-eyed at the train station in Newcastle as Mike and I waited to board the train for London. Mike commented that I had planned the trip and could have arranged for us to stay longer. When we arrived at our hotel in London, he called Carly. Mike is now married to Jennifer and is the father of two. Carly became a lawyer and is also married.

I took young Rob on many trips to San Francisco, stopping in Monterey on the way or putting up a tent at Morro Bay and sleeping on the beach. We went to Washington and spent a couple weeks with relatives in Kirkland, across the Evergreen Point Floating Bridge from Seattle. When I returned to Los Angeles and my job at MacGregor's Sporting Goods after that trip, MacGregor's management announced the company was leaving LA and moving to Whittier. I could either move with them or find another job closer to home. Although I contemplated moving to Kirkland, my friend Margaret, from Scotland, had recently joined CBS's legal department and suggested I apply for a secretarial job at CBS Television City in LA.

Chapter 9

The Beginning of a New Era

I phoned CBS personnel and got an appointment to take the standard typing test and meet with the head of the department that had the open secretarial position. The story of this interview leaves people shaking their heads in disbelief. The man I interviewed with asked if I planned to have another child. Since I had one young child and was divorced, I answered no. Did I plan to marry again? "Not at this time," I said. Who knew? Then I was asked how I would arrive for work, what route did I drive, and would that be my regular route or did I plan to vary it. These questions were repeated as the man in charge made small circles on his notepad. Not check marks, circles. This, it turned out, was his trademark. After the interview, I didn't hear anything from CBS. After a few days, I decided to phone Mary Albright, director of CBS personnel. I was glad I called. They, meaning the department head and herself, were just waiting to see if I was really interested enough to call. Ms. Albright said I had the job.

I began working in television at a time when a woman was advised if she wanted to be taken seriously, then she should cover her arms. Male anchors wore suits and ties, although beneath the anchor desk, and unseen by viewers, they might be wearing jeans.

CBS Television City, photo courtesy of CBS Alumni

Women wore jackets, with arms covered, or long-sleeved blouses. In those days, women were hired only as secretaries, receptionists, or switchboard operators. There was even a contest that year called Miss CinderEmmy in which women participants, including some from CBS, competed against the other networks for the title. I want to emphasize this was not a bathing suit competition. CBS's Lois O'Connor, a receptionist at Television City who went on to produce programs such as *The Patty Duke Show*, *Get Smart*, and *Playhouse 90*, won Miss CinderEmmy. She married actor Jason Robards several years later.

One KNXT producer, Linda Day, who worked for "Human Predicament" segment reporter Ralph Story, told me about the time she showed up for work wearing a pantsuit. Linda said when she arrived at the Columbia Square artists' entrance, the guard wouldn't admit her to the building because of her outfit. She believes she was the first woman to do so at KNXT. She had to wait outside while the guard called the station's program director to get approval to admit her to the building. Women's rights had not "come a long way, baby" by then. Linda Day went on to become one of the first women directors in Hollywood, with sitcoms *Kate and Allie, Mad About You,* and *Married with Children* among her directorial credits.

Chapter 10

Wake-Up Call

The teenage years are a struggle for many kids and their parents. I felt my son was on a bad path and that something drastic had to be done. One night, when he came home late under the influence I had a very hard decision to make. I told him to get into my car, and I drove him to the Culver City Police Department. The officer on duty suggested I leave him there overnight and that we could meet in the morning. It was the wake-up call my son needed. There was a community effort in Culver City's Police Department to help troubled kids, and they knew Rob had no father around. One of the officers got him into the ride-along program and assured me his night in jail would not appear on his record. It was painful for me to do, but I'm thankful that I did.

I can never thank the Culver City police enough for taking Rob and helping to turn his life around. Rob has never held it against me. In fact, his son, Michael, my grandson, asked me when he was a teenager if it was true that I had had his dad jailed. I think perhaps he was acting up, and Rob suggested to him that he might do the same thing with him that I had done to straighten him out. Rob turned into a wonderful man: educated, responsible, and a great father to two wonderful kids. He's a terrific role model, and I'm very proud of the person he turned out to be. I felt I made the right choice, however difficult, to save my son. It was an agonizing decision that caused me a lot of guilt, but given the circumstances, I made the best decision.

Lake Balboa with grandchildren, Mike and Kim, and son Rob

Chapter 11

Adult Education

I was determined that my son, Rob, should have a good education, the best that I could afford. Also, I decided I'd better set a good example. I returned to school in order to get my high school diploma before he did. Only close friends knew about my past and lack of education. I worked full time at Channel 2 News and attended Culver City High adult education classes four nights a week, making up the three years I'd missed. I passed the GED test and, with pride, had a cap-and-gown graduation ceremony. I continued taking classes at Pepperdine and later at West LA College.

The night classes at Culver provided an interesting side perk. I shared coffee breaks with a classmate, Agnes Bonin. We'd talk about our teenage kids—my Rob, her Mary. They didn't know each other. A few years later, Rob came home one day and said he'd met this great new girl, Mary Bonin. They married a few years after that, and Agnes and I became in-laws. Prior to our graduation, the local *Culver City Star News* sent a reporter and photographer to do a local color piece on some of the graduates. On June 5, 1969, Agnes and I were featured in a front-page story with a picture modeling our caps and gowns. I framed that photo, and our grandchildren enjoy seeing it and hearing about our night school meeting.

Graduation year

Chapter 12

Equality and the Glass Ceiling

There wasn't much talk about parity in the sixties, seventies, and eighties. There simply were not a lot of jobs for women in television, and women made significantly less than their male counterparts. Each department at CBS had an allotted amount for raises. The news director made decisions on percentages of the money fund and which employees got high or low increases in salary. Another woman staffer and I were called in to the news director's office, where he told us we were doing exceptional, outstanding work but that he only had so much money in the department fund to distribute, and he was giving the highest amount to a man in the graphics area because "he's married and has a family." This woman and I were single parents—divorced with no child support—however, we agreed and accepted the news director's explanation. It wasn't until many years later that women began to fight the glass ceiling and push for salary equality.

One news director I worked for had a habit of mixing up staff names and their positions. Paperwork for an evaluation and approval for a sizable raise came through from the Channel 2 business office for a longtime newsman the station had considered deadwood and whom previous news directors had attempted to phase out. He remained, however, and was given an "outstanding" approval and a considerable raise. The news director told me later he had mixed up this person's name with an assignment desk manager whom he considered 100 percent outstanding and to whom he intended to award a big raise. Because of his mistake, he had to reduce the increase for the deserving person.

When I started working at Television City, women were employed as secretaries or receptionists. Department heads were men, with the exception of Ann Nelson, who was director of business affairs for CBS on the West Coast. Ann started her career with CBS in a part-time job in 1945 and remained with the company for sixty-four years. She worked in various positions and was promoted to director of business affairs in 1959. Ann was vocal about her longing to be named a vice president, and forty years later, in 1999, she was promoted to the position. During those forty years, she watched as males with far less tenure were given the VP title. In her position as director, she had negotiated landmark contracts for CBS shows such as *I Love Lucy*, *Gunsmoke*, *All in the Family*, and *The Young and the Restless*. Anne Nelson died in 2009 at age eighty-six, and the mezzanine floor at Television City was dedicated the Ann Nelson Mezzanine.

At KNXT, Channel 2, the same situation occurred with Alberta (Berte) Hackett, director of business affairs for the station and next in line to the general manager. Did she become GM? No. Berte stayed in her position while new male GMs arrived over the years from other cities, in one instance from WBBM, Chicago Radio. Consultants hired by the New York office decided Los Angeles general managers could be transferred from radio and didn't necessarily have to be familiar with the television side of the business. I was happy to be in television news during a time that, although slow in appearing, there were training programs for women technicians, resulting in more being hired. The glass ceiling was challenged, and it was a time of change and growth. Women writers and reporters were added to our staff. Women were promoted to producers and directors. Shortly after I retired, a woman, Nancy Bauer Gonzales, was named news director at Channel 2.

With reporters (L to R) Mary Grady, Pat LaLama, Thelma Gutierrez

Chapter 13

CBS Television City: The Golden Years at the Tiffany Network

During the golden age of television, TV City was an exciting, vibrant place to work. Studios 31, 33, 41, and 43 were situated two on each side of a wide hallway and were the homes to full-time production of *Playhouse 90*, a live television broadcast that turned out the best upcoming directors such as John Frankenheimer and shows such as *Requiem for a Heavyweight* and *Days of Wine and Roses*. Frankenheimer was a perfectionist in that he wanted everything on his set to go right. He wanted a water tank built for a *Playhouse 90* "Old Man" episode, starring actor Sterling Hayden. Since the studio couldn't hold the huge and heavy tank, it was placed in the center hallway between Studios 31 and 33 and cracked the floor.

Art Linkletter's *House Party, Climax!* and Red Skelton's comedy show were in the other three studios. Employees nicknamed Skelton's show rehearsal "the dirty hour"; we, lunchtime permitting, could sit in the audience section to watch. Red loved having us there. He enjoyed wisecracking and ad-libbing and was such a lovely guy, beloved by everyone. His guest stars read like a Hollywood Who's Who. Once, entering the studio through a hall door, I heard a voice behind me. Startled, I turned and looked to see actor Errol Flynn, who said, "Not able to swing in the trees anymore." His appearance was, in fact, alarming; he had gained considerable weight, and his face was puffy. Errol Flynn died shortly after his appearance on Red's show.

Red also had actress Jayne Mansfield on the show. During rehearsal, the two got raucous, Jayne keeping up with him laugh for laugh, telling dirty jokes that were, of course, not in the script. When extras from *Playhouse 90* learned current sexy film favorite Jayne Mansfield was next door, the entire group decked out in military uniforms came over to sit in on rehearsal. Red and Jayne enjoyed having them in the audience and played off the howling laughter. Finally, the director asked that the studio be cleared so that the "real rehearsal" of Red's show could take place. It was an experience none of us sitting in during that "dirty hour" will ever forget.

In 1963, Judy Garland was hired by CBS to do a variety-type show. The show's producers asked that a trailer be purchased and brought into Television City for Judy's use. The trailer was hauled up the side of the TV City building and brought through the west side, where windows had been removed to allow it to be pulled into the building and placed at the end of the center studio hallway near the elevator. A yellow brick road was painted on the floor leading from the trailer entrance to the Studio 33 entrance on the same level. At Judy's request, the interior of the trailer was decorated in white— white furniture and white carpeting. I'd seen Judy at a sold-out concert at the Greek Theatre and thought she gave the best performance I'd ever seen, deserving of the critical acclaim it received. She was amazing in person. And there I was, walking behind her in a hallway at TV City. She was small and thin, and what I noted most was her legs, which were so slim they looked like they could hardly support her. But her walk was another thing. She walked with a purpose.

She wanted to see that the show she signed on to do became a hit. CBS employees were sometimes able to eat lunch in the studio area of Judy's show during rehearsals, but the set was not as open as Skelton's. Depending on the Garland show guests, her director (or Judy's mood) determined whether it would be OK to enter the rehearsal and observe. One such occasion was during a young, upcoming singer's rehearsal—Barbra Streisand—who was, and still is, amazing. I got to watch and hear her and Judy rehearse "Happy Days Are Here Again," an experience I'll never forget. I was already a fan of Judy's, and that day, I became a fan of Barbra's. Another time, a teenage Liza Minnelli walked down the Television City hallway arm in arm with her mother. She was making her first professional television appearance on Judy's show. In childhood, Liza appeared in the movie *Gigi*, directed by her father, Vincent Minnelli.

I was offered a position as secretary to the Garland show writers. I was told, however, that the last person hired in the program department would be the first to be let go if a show faced cancellation. I needed a secure position because I was supporting a child and couldn't afford to be laid off, so I turned down the Garland show offer and decided to wait it out until a news position opened. Later, CBS canceled the Garland program. I must add here that, despite using the term *show* in my story, during my early years at CBS Television City, there was a directive from the program director stating that William Paley, owner of CBS (often dubbed the Tiffany Network because of its high standards and quality programming), did not like the term *show* used. CBS had television broadcasts or programs, not shows.

I saw many upcoming actors and actresses during my six years at CBS Television City. Some were memorable, such as young Canadian actor William Shatner. We seemed to have the same arrival time, and I would see him in the parking lot or at the artists' entrance each day. Shatner was working on a live production, "A Town That Turned to Dust," for the weekly CBS broadcast show *Climax!*

In 1958, Steve McQueen guest starred in an episode of *Climax!* The often-repeated story about him tearing down his photo from the hallway entrance at Television City is true. He simply didn't like the picture. McQueen starred in *Wanted: Dead or Alive.* The show was popular with fans, and McQueen was a rising star. In those days, he was known to have a bit of a temper, but CBS was willing to overlook it. He also didn't think the assigned spaces in the Television City parking lot applied to him. He would be admitted at the gate entrance and then speed to just in front of the stairs leading to the artists' entrance, slam on his brakes, and jump out, leaving the car not in a space but right where everyone had to walk around it to reach the stairs. But Steve McQueen's talent was obvious. He went on to become a big star in films such as *Bullitt* and *The Great Escape.*

At the back of Television City was the "lunch truck" operated by Lou Rose. The truck, or wagon, sat just below a ramp leading into the sets area, and on the other side of the wagon was the gate leading to the Farmers' Market, now expanded to include the Grove shops, theater, and entertainment center. Everybody working at TV City went to Lou's truck or walked across to the Farmers' Market to grab a bite from one of the many vendors and sit outside under the trees. On breaks, I sat beside Joanne Woodward and Paul Newman, just dating at the time and costars on *Playhouse 90*'s "The 80 Yard Run," and character actor Peter Lorre and actress Eva Marie Saint. One morning, I was sitting on a bench near the lunch truck having coffee when I heard a man's deep voice ask if he might join me. To my surprise, it was actor Boris Karloff. He was distinguished and nice looking, actually quite handsome—a change from his famous on-screen portrayal of Frankenstein's monster in a series of successful films. He was on a break from rehearsal of *Playhouse 90*. I was so in awe I couldn't say much.

Shortly after I began working at Television City on Beverly Boulevard, Elvis Presley announced he would be making a two-night concert appearance next door at the Pan Pacific Auditorium. A friend in CBS's publicity department had tickets and invited me to attend. The date was October 28, 1957. Elvis performed his well-known hits, including "Hound Dog," complete with gyrating hips. Girls screamed and cried during the concert. His performance was terrific! Seeing the King of Rock and Roll in person and hearing him live was beyond any earlier television appearances I'd seen, although some reviewers considered his act too racy. After the show, when we were walking from the auditorium to our car, we heard what sounded like a stampede behind us. Elvis's fans were running after his departing car. We ran to get out of the way. Press coverage of Elvis's hip-swiveling performance caught the attention of the Los Angeles police, who sent investigators to his second night's performance on October 29. He toned it down somewhat from what we'd seen the night before, and police allowed the show to go on.

Years later, on August 16, 1977, my news director boss at Channel 2 stepped out of his office and asked me to call Ed Hookstratten, Elvis Presley's lawyer and agent, and tell him Channel 2 News got a report Elvis had died. He wanted to know if Hookstratten could confirm before we went to air. I knew Hookstratten well, as he represented many of our Channel 2 on-air talent. He would not confirm the report at that time. The news of Elvis's death at his home at Graceland in Memphis was later broadcast as breaking news worldwide. He collapsed in his bathroom and was rushed to a Memphis hospital, where he was pronounced dead.

Chapter 14

Infamous Cases in LA News History

As a young adult, I followed some infamous murderer cases in Southern California. One was the case of Barbara Graham, whose trial was covered extensively by newspapers and television. Graham was only thirty-one years old when she was arrested and charged with the murder of Mabel Monahan of Burbank on March 9, 1953, the year my son, Rob, was born. Two thugs Graham had hooked up with had convinced her that Monahan, age sixty-four, had a sizable stash of money and jewelry in her Burbank home. Graham went to Monahan's door and lied her way into the house, saying she needed to use a phone. Her partners, Jack Santo and Emmett Perkins, rushed in after Graham gained access. Graham reportedly pistol-whipped Monahan, cracking her skull. The three then suffocated her with a pillow. They escaped with nothing of value; her purse, containing money and some jewelry, was found later by police in a nearby closet. Santo, Perkins, and Graham were convicted of murder and executed in California's gas chamber on June 3, 1955. The story of Barbara Graham was made into a 1958 film, *I Want to Live*, starring actress Susan Hayward and directed by Robert Wise. The movie received six Oscars. Susan Hayward won the Best

Actress Oscar for her portrayal of Graham. Robert Wise won an Oscar and the Directors Guild of America Award for Direction.

Around the time I began working at TV City in the mid-1950s, there was another intriguing story—that of L. Ewing Scott and his wealthy wife, Evelyn Throsby Scott, who lived in the upscale west side Bel Air community, a suburb of Los Angeles. They had been married five years when Evelyn went missing in 1955. It was an era before recycling and trash truck pick up; Los Angeles and its suburbs had backyard incinerators. Investigators on the scene found Evelyn's eyeglasses and dentures in the ashes near the Scotts' incinerator. But Evelyn's body was not found. One rumor theorized that she disappeared the night concrete and foundation was being poured for the new section of the 405 (the San Diego freeway), which ran near the Los Angeles suburb of Brentwood. When asked, Scott would only laugh and respond, "If they think that, let 'em dig up the freeway." Scott was indicted by a Los Angeles grand jury and fled to Canada. He was arrested when he left Canada to buy a car in Detroit. A jury convicted Scott in 1959 despite no body being found. His case became the first in US history of conviction using circumstantial evidence and was termed "the no-body trial." The jury rejected the death penalty and voted for life in prison. Many years later, when I was working at KNXT, Channel 2 News with reporter Bill Stout, I mentioned the L. Ewing Scott case and my thought that Stout should try to interview him in San Quentin prison. Stout loved the idea. He had covered the trial and found it a fascinating case, as I did. We were successful in getting a jailhouse interview. Still holding fast, Scott would admit to nothing. Stout ended the interview by offering to take Scott to dinner at Chasen's if and when he was paroled—Chasen's was an upscale west side restaurant Scott and Evelyn frequented during their marriage. Scott was offered parole in 1974, but declined, saying he was wrongfully held. He was released from prison in 1978.

Writer Diane Wagner followed his case over the years and stayed in touch with him. Scott phoned Wagner and asked to meet. According to a *Los Angeles Times* article, Scott confessed to Wagner, thirty years after the crime. She accomplished what no one had been able to do. He admitted he had murdered Evelyn and transported her body to the Las Vegas desert and buried it. Diane Wagner wrote a book, *Corpus Delecti: True Story of L. Ewing Scott Convicted of Murder without Corpse or Confession*. L. Ewing Scott died penniless at age ninety-one on August 17, 1987.

One more infamous murder case and trial I followed closely while I was working as a secretary at Television City was the Finch/Tregoff story. Prominent LA surgeon Dr. Bernard Finch, forty-one, was carrying on an extramarital affair with his receptionist, twenty-year-old Carole Tregoff, also married. In September 1958, Barbara Finch discovered her husband's affair and phoned Tregoff's husband, Jimmy Pappa. Tregoff filed for divorce from Pappa, her high school sweetheart, but if Finch filed for divorce from Barbara, then she could clean him out. Finch and Tregoff traveled from West Covina and met up in Las Vegas, where Tregoff hired ex-con John Patrick Cody and gave him a down payment of $350 to kill Barbara Finch. When Cody returned, he informed Tregoff the job was done; however, she learned Barbara was still alive after she paid Cody the balance of $850. Tregoff and Finch traveled back to West Covina to take action themselves—the two waited outside the Finch home on July 18, 1959, watching for Barbara to arrive. The Finch's maid heard screams and ran out to the garage, where Finch shot at her. She testified that Dr. Finch hit her head with his fists, but she was able to break away and run back into the house to call the police. Barbara Finch was shot and killed instantly. Tregoff and Finch fled to Vegas, where they were captured. Both claimed Barbara drew a gun and was killed during a scuffle. The first trial ended in a hung jury. The second trial, in 1961, ended in first-degree convictions and sentencing to life in prison. Carole Tregoff served eight years before parole; she changed her name and moved away. Dr. Finch served ten years and was paroled, moved to another state, had his medical license reinstated, and remarried. He died in 1995 at age seventy-seven.

Another story that captured my attention was that of Elizabeth "Ma" Duncan, who hired two men to kill her pregnant daughter-in-law, Olga, whom she hated The press nicknamed Mrs. Duncan "Ma". Duncan hated anyone who came between her and her lawyer son, Frank. Augustine Baldonado confessed that Duncan offered him and Luis Moya $6,000 to kill Olga. The two men led authorities to Olga's body, buried in Ventura County. She had been kidnapped, beaten, raped, and possibly buried alive. During her effort to break up her son's marriage, Duncan had illegally obtained an annulment of Frank and Olga's marriage. I was working at CBS Television City when Baldonado, Moya, and Duncan were executed in California's gas chamber on the same day, August 8, 1962. "Ma" was fifty-eight years old. At her execution, she asked, "Where's Frank? I am innocent." Frank was working on getting his mother's execution delayed. He was in San Francisco pleading her case before the US Court of Appeals. The court refused the plea.

Several years later, when I was working in news at Channel 2, there was an execution scheduled at San Quentin; it had been some years since an execution had taken place in California. I thought back to Frank Duncan and decided it would be worth the effort to find him to see if he would do an interview about the death penalty. He was still practicing law. I obtained a phone number and made the call. I started to tell the person on the line what I was phoning about, and to my surprise, he had answered the phone himself. He said, "Well, you found me. I'm not going to do an interview. I have never done interviews. I won't do one now." He was gracious about it, but determined.

Chapter 15

Entering the Political Arena

I hadn't given politics much thought until John F. Kennedy. Like many in my age group in the 1960s, the US senator from Massachusetts captured my hopes and dreams for the future. He was young, only forty-three, while his opponent, Richard Nixon, was forty-seven but seemed much older. Kennedy was energetic and youthful and had a relaxed, informal style. I took my son, Rob, to see Kennedy when he arrived by plane at LA's West Imperial Terminal, south of LAX. There was a small crowd in attendance as Kennedy disembarked the airplane, climbed on top of a waiting sedan, and waved to our group, shaking hands before the car left the tarmac. He was even more charismatic in person than on television.

The Democratic Convention was held at Los Angeles Memorial Sports Arena from July 11–15, 1960. The CBS News broadcast area was in need of a receptionist, and I was tapped to work one of the four days. There were no other jobs for women, so I gladly put on the corsage I was given to wear while at the CBS News reception desk. I was thrilled to be any part of the convention coverage. A good part of my day was spent directing male guests to the men's room.

When I worked in John Kennedy's campaign as an unpaid volunteer, I was employed by CBS Television but not in the news department. (Under CBS policy, news personnel are not permitted to work in political campaigns.) During the campaign, my volunteer duties included going door-to-door, ringing doorbells in LA's Fairfax district not far from CBS Television City. As a result of my volunteering, I was invited to a party at the home of actor Barry Sullivan. Sullivan's daughter Jenny and her friend entertained by singing. Among the guests were actress Esther Williams and actor Fernando Lamas. I was surprised when Ted Kennedy, JFK's youngest brother, arrived and greeted each one of us personally and thanked us for helping with his brother's campaign. I got his autograph on an anti-Nixon for president campaign flier.

John Kennedy picked Texas Senator Lyndon B. Johnson to be his vice-presidential running mate; Republican candidate Richard Nixon picked Ambassador Henry Cabot Lodge as his. Not long after, I was standing in the CBS Television City center hall waiting for the elevator when a very distinguished gentleman approached me. He was alone. This was before the days of heavy security. He introduced himself by saying, "Hello. My name is Henry Cabot Lodge, and I am running for the office of vice president." He was at TV City for a sit-down television interview.

The presidential election of 1960 was a first in that Kennedy was the youngest candidate and also a Catholic. Being Catholic myself, I was distressed to find anti-Catholic, anti-Kennedy fliers on cars parked in the CBS employees' parking lot and posted in the CBS ladies' room. However, John Kennedy won the democratic nomination and the presidency despite anti-Catholic sentiments.

Chapter 16

Television City to KNXT
at Columbia Square

I worked at Television City for six years, always hoping to get into the network news bureau based there. I made friends with correspondents Harold Dow and Charles Kuralt, both supportive of my desire to join news, and I talked to the bureau chief, Bob Schakne, several times—I was a pest, as a matter of fact—but there was one woman in the LA bureau office, a secretary, and that wasn't going to change. Then one day, I saw a job posted for local news at KNXT, Channel 2, located at Columbia Square on Sunset Boulevard and Gower in Hollywood. I applied and was interviewed and hired by news director Roy Heatly. I joined office administrator Bette Penny as one of only two women in news. When I told my boss, Leo Gregory, at Television City I was leaving to join the Channel 2 News team, he said he was sorry to see me go but glad I applied for the news job and got it. He knew I wanted to work in news and how limited the jobs were for women. He also gave me some advice: "Don't be so serious, laugh, lighten up, and don't approach things apologetically."

Robert "Bob" Wood was the general manager at KNXT, and *The Big News*, anchored by Jerry Dunphy, had started in 1961. KNXT's

The Big News was a nightly viewing habit. I felt the news team of Jerry Dunphy, Maury Green, Paul Udell, John Hart, Ralph Story, Gil Stratton, and Bill Keene were like family coming into my home. I knew them before I walked into the newsroom for my job interview. I joined *The Big News* team, consisting of forty-two white males, on October 22, 1963.

Chapter 17

The Assassination of John F. Kennedy

On November 22, 1963, President John F. Kennedy was assassinated in Dallas, Texas. I had joined KNXT, Channel 2, just one month earlier. The news of his assassination was devastating, and it shocked the country. I had never considered the possibility of assassination, though I'd heard the term when I was growing up. My grandmother, born in 1885, would talk about President McKinley's assassination on September 6, 1901, which she recalled in detail.

The television news bulletin first flashed during the CBS soap opera *As the World Turns*; it was audio only, since cameras had not been set up for a live report. The network cut in to regular programming with anchor Walter Cronkite, at that time the most trusted man in America, giving the heartbreaking news, first of Kennedy's grave condition, and soon after, the news that the president had died. Cronkite's face, and the tone of his voice, said it all when his news bulletin to the country read: "President Kennedy died at one o'clock in the afternoon central standard time."

Wire services AP and UPI were sending bulletin sound alarms, and our writers and producers were rushing to write updates for Channel 2's live coverage. Correspondent John Hart was sent from

Los Angeles to Dallas. Cots were brought into the newsroom so staff could rest during long working hours. All TV commercials were canceled. The newsroom phones were swamped with calls from viewers asking in disbelief if the news of the assassination was, in fact, true. When I answered my phone, I had an interoffice CBS call from Television City; it was actor/comedian Danny Kaye on the line, calling from his dressing room. Kaye was doing a weekly comedy show at TV City. He wanted me to confirm that the bulletin he had just seen on his monitor was accurate. I told him sadly that it was. Kaye didn't say a word. He hung up in shock.

My ten-year-old son, Rob, was in school, and the nuns at Saint Augustine's in Culver City sent all the children home. We lived with my grandmother, so I knew he was safe at home while I worked long hours at the station. It was nonstop in the newsroom for three days: first the assassination, and then the shocking live coverage of captured suspected assassin Lee Harvey Oswald, who was shot and killed by Jack Ruby two days later on November 24, 1963. Ruby, a Dallas nightclub owner, made his way into the police station basement tunnel where Oswald, in police custody, was being transferred by authorities. Several reporters were standing nearby to observe the transfer. Suddenly, Jack Ruby stepped out from the crowd, gun drawn, and approached Oswald, fatally shooting him on live TV. Commercial-free television coverage continued 24-7 up to and following the president's funeral.

On Monday, November 25, 1963, we aired live "Human Predicament" by reporter Ralph Story." Story was a regular on *The Big News* and his "Human Predicaments" were nightly features, often about LA locals or some development on the national scene. The feature for November 25, however, was about the most tragic incident in the nation. Nate Kaplan, who writes brilliantly and from the heart, wrote the piece that turned out later to be the most requested script copy from viewers. His subject was then-three-year-old John Kennedy Jr., whose father had been assassinated. As delivered by Ralph Story and written by Nate Kaplan:

He is three years old and it is his birthday, but it is not like a birthday at all. His father is not there, and his mother who is beautiful and laughs a lot and loves colors is dressed in dark clothes, and does not laugh and many grown-ups come and talk to her and they do not laugh either. The other children who play with him in the playground are not here today, though they were supposed to be. Don't they know it's his birthday? Instead of the children and the cake and the party, there are the grownups dressed in dark clothes, coming and going in big, black cars. It is not Sunday, it is his birthday, but they are going to church—he and his mother and sister and all the big quiet people. And he must do as he is told because there is something different and strange about today. He can feel it, though he is not quite sure what it is, except that it has something to do with his father. There are many people at the church whom he does not usually see there, and they do not smile and wink at him as they do when his daddy is with him and they go up the steps and down the aisle together. Back home the hallways are empty and silent where his father used to shout, "Where are my rascals?" and he and his sister would come running. He and his sister will have to stay here now while their mother goes out without them. And he can look again at the flag the man gave him yesterday where all the people and so many flags were, when he said: "I want a flag to take home to my daddy." When his mother comes back she can only give him a very little attention because of how many people are there in the house, some in soldier suits and some in funny clothes that look like they were meant for a party, but he can tell they are not. And why isn't his father there, who is always there with his mother when there are strange big people downstairs in the big house? It is not like a birthday, and he does not understand. He will understand on some tomorrow, but this is today and his father is not here. A bad man killed his father, yes, but why isn't his father here? And there is no answer. For who can explain to a three-year-old boy on his birthday that his father is now a flame that burns eternally in the place across the river where the soldiers are?

I typed teleprompter during my first months at Channel 2, and heartbroken over Kennedy's assassination, it was difficult to get through typing Nate's piece, but like everyone on the staff, I needed to get the script ready for air fast. I worked those sad days with a heavy heart and a lump in my throat.

On Presidents' Day, February 20, 1989, the Dallas museum dedicated to President Kennedy opened on the sixth floor of the former School Book Depository. In 1991, when my son and his family lived near Dallas, I visited them, and my daughter-in-law, Mary, took my grandchildren, Kim and Mike, and me to the scene of Kennedy's assassination at Dealey Plaza and the Texas School Book Depository. I found the perspective as far as the distance that I'd seen in television footage to be different; looking out the sixth-floor window where assassin Oswald had pointed his rifle at Kennedy's motorcade seemed not the great distance I had pictured from news reports in 1963. Standing in Dealey Plaza near the grassy knoll and noticing the silence of other visitors at the scene was an experience I won't forget.

Chapter 18

New in the Newsroom

When I moved from CBS Television City to KNXT, the local CBS news station in Hollywood, *The Big News* was the highest-rated news program in Los Angeles, and I, like most of LA's population, was a viewer. I was eager, excited, and anxious about meeting the news staff on my first day; plus, I was entering the Columbia Square artists' entrance, a hallowed place I'd come to know as a kid growing up in Hollywood. I went from standing outside in the same parking lot on Sundays as a young fan to entering the cherished doorway as a young adult. I didn't know what to expect. This was a news broadcast I had been viewing since its inception in 1961. My first days in the newsroom were intimidating. I became the news director's person, the news administrator, and did payroll every Monday, performed secretarial duties, took dictation, and answered phones and viewer mail. I typed teleprompter for the news broadcast. The teleprompter was typed on yellow paper in large black type. Every so often, a letter would break on the teleprompter typewriter, and I would use a large black marking pen to write in the missing letters. When late copy came, I would run to the studio and give it to a stage manager, who then ran it over to the studio person operating the teleprompter in front of the anchors. I held the longevity record as secretary to the news director, holding the position from 1963 to 1982. As personal assistant, I was the confidential ears and eyes during a time when the station was number one in the market, and I also later witnessed its later slide in the ratings when it became third.

Working at KNXT

One of the first people I met at Columbia Square was KNX Radio host Bob Crane. I didn't know anyone outside the newsroom and would sit outside in the courtyard to eat my lunch. Crane came up to me, introduced himself, and welcomed me to the Columbia

Square family. His radio broadcast was done on the opposite side of the building from our television newsroom. Bob Crane went on to television and starred in the popular hit *Hogan's Heroes*. Several years later, in 1978, I would be working on a tragic news story about his murder, which has never been solved.

Over the years, some others who came through the artists' entrance door at Columbia Square to work with me at KNXT (later KCBS) were Ann Curry, Lester Holt, Brent Musberger, Jim Lampley, Bree Walker, Pat O'Brien, Connie Chung, Paula Zahn, Penny Griego, Maury Povich, Drew Griffin, Ross Becker, Hosea Sanders, Steve Kmetko, Harvey Levin, Steve Hartman, and David Sheehan.

With anchor Penny Griego

With entertainment reporter Steve Kmetko

Chapter 19

The Captain and His (News) Crew

There is a reason Channel 2 was number one. It was a team. On a daily basis, producer Pete Noyes, affectionately known as "the captain," was heard shouting at the top of his voice, "I'm the captain of this ship. When I say write it this way, you damn well better write it this way," all while jumping up and standing on his desk, his long shirttail out and flapping as he gestured. Pete would always be right, of course, and the proof was the production of the best newscast in the country. Roy Heatly held the title of news director, but it was Pete who led the successful *Big News* team of writers, producers, and on-air talent. He was a legend in the Los Angeles news business even then, colorful and boisterous. It seemed every payday, someone would lose a paycheck; most often it was Pete. Wastebaskets would be turned over in the search to retrieve a check. When Pete elected to leave Channel 2 News to join our competition across town at KABC, we threw a going-away party for him. As a goodbye gag gift, I went out and bought a men's shirt with the longest shirttail I could find. He wrote a goodbye memo to the staff that ended with the saying, "Your picture will always be on my piano." Several years later, Pete and I worked together again. He returned to Channel 2

News to work on investigations; Pete was not only great at producing investigative pieces but also the best in town. He had developed
valuable contacts within law enforcement. He did a lot of digging.
He got tips from his sources. No one in town could touch him. Pete
has never really retired; he's writing books these days (*Who Killed the
Big News?*) and is still wiser than anyone in the business.

When I first joined *The Big News* in 1963, Georges Fischer and
Chuck Riley manned the assignment desk, two men sharing one
work space. It was amazing to watch those two at work. Fischer and
Riley had between them multiple sources and tipsters, and camera
crews and reporters could be dispatched quickly. Wire machines
were the information highway—no social media, no bloggers. City
News Service (CNS), Associated Press (AP), and United Press
International (UPI) provided the releases. (Anchorman Baxter
Ward at KABC Channel 7 actually did rip and read wire copy during live broadcasts.) Georges Fischer, who had complete command
over breaking news as well as the day-to-day general assignment
stories, would answer the phone and yell "FISH…ERR," at the
same time spilling his coffee on a desk-size blotter. As the new
member, I would grab a clean blotter and slip it onto Fischer's
desk.

Producers Pat O'Reilly and Jim Vinson also worked the
desk. Mike Daniels produced the 11:00 p.m. broadcast, with Al
Greenstein as editor. And *The Big News* had some of the best young
news writers in the business: Joe Saltzman, David Browning, Bob
Flick, and Joe Dyer, who was the first African American news
writer to join the team. Once when taking dictation from assistant
news director Patrick O'Reilly, I recall typing his directive to our
Big News writers: "Never use the phrase 'Needless to say' in your
news copy. Why? Because O'Reilly said, 'If it's needless to say, then
why say it.'"

Saul Halpert and Jim Brown were general assignment reporters. Saul was my go-to guy when I needed the definition of a word I didn't understand, which often occurred when I took dictation and was too embarrassed to ask the person dictating. One word I recall to this day is *tantamount*. I was handed that one during dictation from one of our anchors. Saul gave me the definition and kept my inquiry confidential.

If the news assignment desk doesn't function efficiently or have the right staff, then nothing works, and KNXT Channel 2's was the envy of Los Angeles television news departments. Following the conversion of Columbia Records recording studio to a new newsroom for KNXT, our assignment desk was in an area near the edit rooms and the planning desk, the very best in the business. I have to lead off with the much-loved Steve Crawford. If he didn't give you the finger when you were walking toward him at the assignment desk, then you felt maybe he didn't like you. It was the compliment of the day!

Assignment editor Steve Crawford

The desk was crewed by a long list of pros, including Bob Long, Bob Harmon, Jose Rios, Hans Laetz, Jack Fox, Rubin Green, Jeff Wald, Steve Bien, and Rod Foster. Jack Noyes, Jacki Wells, Dree Declamacy, Sy Kravitz, Rosalva Skidmore, MaryHelen Campa, Terry Doyle, and planning directors Nan Tepper and Akila Gibbs, along with assistants Cecelia Alvear and Margie Friedman, handled day-to-day scheduling of our coverage of planned news events based on press releases or telephone tips.

Chapter 20

Bob Wood: KNXT's Most Beloved General Manager

We were number one in the ratings with *The Big News*, in part because of Bob Wood's influence. Wood was supportive, mingled with the news and station staff, and came into the newsroom often just to chat. He threw parties for the staff, whether for special occasions such as end of sweeps or for no occasion at all. He raised morale just by being present. A USC graduate, he hired the team's marching band to come into the station and march up and down the center hallway and out onto Sunset Boulevard; they marched around the corner at Columbia Square and into the parking lot behind the building. Traffic stopped on Sunset while motorists listened to and watched the USC Trojans in their red-and-gold regalia.

Bob left KNXT in 1969 to become president of CBS in New York. During his tenure as network president, he brought to television some of its biggest ratings hits, such as *The Mary Tyler Moore Show*, *MASH*, and *All in the Family*. When he came back to visit the station a few years later and was met by overwhelming applause, he jumped up on one of the desks and gave an impromptu pep talk to employees, most of whom he remembered and addressed by their first names. Wood knew more of our names than the current general manager, who was too vain to wear his glasses and didn't recognize any of us. (In fact, when he left his office, he would ask his secretary to accompany him, so she could whisper the name of anyone he might encounter. She even made him a photo album with all our pictures in it.)

Bob Wood died May 22, 1986. I attended his funeral at All Saints Episcopal in Beverly Hills. It was the largest memorial service I'd ever attended, with standing-room only. Comedians Bob Newhart and Don Rickles, together at the microphone, presented eulogies. It turned out to be a roast, with those two telling hilarious stories about Wood and their time spent together. One story described them all coming back from a night out and crawling up the driveway to Wood's home. Laughter coming from the church could be heard outside on Santa Monica Boulevard.

Chapter 21

Grant Holcomb: News Director, Teacher, Friend

It was Bob Wood who named political correspondent Grant Holcomb news director, to replace Roy Heatly. Wood was tired of answering viewer mail complaining that Grant's reporting was too much to the left in his political coverage. When Grant became news director, he would no longer be on the air. Wood's thought was that *The Big News* would remain a solid number one with Grant at the helm; no Los Angeles television station even came close to challenging Channel 2.

After six years of the payroll/dictation/prompter job, I was working as secretary to news director Grant Holcomb. The Monday payroll was becoming too much. It became necessary for me to work on Sunday. That meant less time with my son. Grant decided to hire another woman, Carole Gardner. She became more than a payroll clerk; she took over the business end of the news department, and we became best friends and worked together until we retired. (Later, more women joined the department, including Liz Mitchell, who teamed with Ralph Story on research. Channel 2 News established training programs for women technicians. In later years, secretaries Cindy Sanders and Shari Freis joined the staff. More progress occurred with the hiring of women news writers, among them Mimi Toberman, Lois Pitter Bruce, Kathy Leverett, Hilary Atkin, Celeste Durant, Rose Krupp, and Tammy Taylor.)

Grant Holcomb was popular among the staff. He never said an unkind word about anyone. Grant came from a well-respected Pasadena, California, family. He had two brothers, one of whom was mayor of San Bernardino. The other was a Broadway show producer. And Grant was a longtime Los Angeles broadcaster. He was the kindest, most caring person I ever worked for. Even when he would tell me about a member of our news staff he didn't particularly like, he was never unkind toward him or her. When the AFTRA (American Federation of Radio and Television Artists) strike occurred and on-air talent was picketing outside the station along Sunset Boulevard, Grant had gourmet food prepared and delivered to the strikers. He sent gift baskets to their homes. The AFTRA strike was so friendly that after it was over, the striking talent threw a party for news management, many of whom were on-air replacements for the talent who had walked out.

News Director Grant Holcomb

During the time Grant was a reporter, he told some funny stories about political campaign trips. He kept a box of different-colored ribbons in his desk drawer, the type to which press passes would be attached. He would be granted travel on a press plane with a candidate by learning ahead what colored ribbon was used for the day and inserting the ribbon in his suit jacket pocket so just enough showed for him to board the plane. The press secretary would be counting the number of reporters and would always be one over, never figuring out it was Grant.

Grant Holcomb called every woman "Honey." He had a problem remembering names. When he would call out from his office, "Oh, honey," three of us would stand up: Carole Gardner, producer Nan Tepper, and me. On many an occasion, he would have a business meeting at a restaurant, and I could count on getting a phone call asking, "Honey, what's the name of this guy I'm having lunch with?" In one instance, when we needed to hire a per diem temporary reporter to cover vacation periods, he handed me a phone number and said, "Honey, call this guy and ask him to come in to work." Later, Grant and I were sitting in his office watching our *Big News* broadcast when the temp reporter appeared. Grant turned to me and said, "Honey, that's the wrong guy." He had gotten the name mixed up.

KNXT, Channel 2 News had one woman reporter, Ruth Ashton Taylor, at that time. Grant interviewed Kelly Lange, who was a helicopter traffic radio reporter. He asked me to produce a television audition with Kelly in-studio. Grant looked at her audition and told her, "Honey, you're very good, but we already have our girl"—the "girl" being Ruth Ashton Taylor. He had one woman reporter on staff, and he was not going to hire another one. Kelly Lange was hired by KNBC, Channel 4 as the on-air TV weather girl, later moving up to anchor of the nightly news broadcasts. Lange was a featured speaker before women's groups and always told the Holcomb "You're very good, but we already have our girl" story. She would ask me to stand up and introduce me, saying, "Lorraine was there. She knows it's true!" Several years passed before a second woman reporter was hired. When Ruth joined the all-male *Big News* team, she didn't just do women's issue stories such as "What's the best makeup?" or medical stories. She covered breaking news: fires, floods, accidents, and crime. Storm coverage found her right in the midst, wearing knee-high boots, wind-blown and fearless. When she married news cameraman Jack Taylor, I attended their wedding. Ruth and Jack Taylor worked as a team, covering stories and winning journalism awards. I had occasion to speak to Ruth Taylor, longtime reporter and the first woman reporter, at Channel 2. I started to tell Ruth about working at ABC News with two sons of former CBS News executives we both knew. Her response was, "And where are the daughters?"

I loved working for Grant as his secretary, his administrative assistant, and his person. He taught me everything about LA politics, California politics, and most importantly, national politics. He knew everyone. Past and present presidents, governors, and congressmen contacted him while I was working for him. He always had something to tell me about each caller or visitor to his office, a humorous tidbit that had never been reported by the media but was something he had personally witnessed. It was my privilege to cover for him when he would often disappear from the news director's office for a few hours. He gave me telephone numbers where I could find him if the general manager needed to speak with him. He loved a couple of restaurants on the Sunset Strip—Scandia and Cock 'n Bull—or he would go across the street on Gower to the Naples, the local watering hole and Channel 2 hangout. Conducting business, he claimed. I never told anyone where he was when I was asked. But if I determined Grant should know about something, then I phoned him. June, the hostess at Scandia, knew I wouldn't try to reach Grant unless it was important.

When CBS management wanted to change news directors, Grant was offered and accepted the position of CBS-owned-and-operated station bureau chief in Washington, DC. We would work together again when he asked me to join him in Miami to cover the Nixon Republican Convention. I later visited Grant and his wife, Jeanne, in Washington, DC, and he took me on a tour. He knew everyone on a first-name basis. Senators and congressmen spoke to him as we toured. On one occasion, a famous congresswoman came up to Grant and greeted him warmly. After she walked away, Grant whispered to me, "Don't tell Jeanne, but if something happens to her, that congresswoman is going to be my next wife." He had a great sense of humor and a quick wit.

Grant's wife, Jeanne, shared with me an example of Grant's humor. She said they attended the opening of an art museum. They were walking from one art exhibit to another when suddenly Grant stopped and stared at a door marked "Fire Exit." He did this for several minutes, with a small crowd gathering behind him, everyone staring up at the fire exit sign. Grant had the group convinced it was a modern art exhibit he was exclaiming about. When my teenage son, Rob, made a trip to DC with his friend Melinda, Grant loved taking them on a tour to see the monuments and to observe Congress in session. He enjoyed seeing their enthusiasm and to be able to share some experiences with them.

Grant died of emphysema. His memorial service was held at All Saints Episcopal Church in Pasadena. Anchormen Jerry Dunphy and Clete Roberts escorted me to the service.

Chapter 22

Clarence Stan Duke: Newsmaker in the Newsroom

Clarence Stan Duke was hired in 1968 as weekend sportscaster. News director Grant Holcomb saw promise in the young African American and added him to the broadcast anchored by long-time Los Angeles newsman Clete Roberts. Years later, following the 11:00 p.m. broadcast on February 9, 1971, Stan, then separated from his wife, Faye, drove by her home, looked into a window, and saw her with Averill Berman, a local radio broadcaster. Stan drove to his home and got his rifle, returned to Faye's home, and shot and killed Berman. I was away for the weekend, having flown to Lake Tahoe with a boyfriend. Upon arrival at Burbank Airport Sunday night, we saw the newspaper headlines: "Stan Duke Arrested for Murder." Monday morning, I learned the desk had tried to reach me because the news director wanted me to iron a shirt for Stan to wear to his arraignment; a producer's wife had fulfilled that task. Stan was represented by famous LA defense attorney Paul Caruso. Grant, Clete, and the station did all they could to support Stan. He was convicted, sentenced, served three years in prison, and paroled in 1974. Stan felt he should get his job back and that his sentence was unfair. He stated he felt he was convicted because he was black and Berman was white, and if it had been the reverse, then no charges would have been filed. He eventually accepted a teaching position at UC Santa Barbara and later attended funeral services for Grant Holcomb held in Pasadena in 1977. Stan Duke died in March 2007 at seventy years old.

Chapter 23

The Big News On-Air

Jerry Dunphy anchored *The Big News*, opening each night's broadcast with "From the desert to the sea to all of Southern California." Jerry had a genuine, warm delivery, a presence, and a voice made for live television. Jerry owned LA; he had a way of touching people through his reading of the news and making viewers feel sympathy or compassion for the situation in which folks found themselves. Jerry also "worked" the community, something Channel 2's competitors didn't take advantage of until years later. He spoke before every group who invited him, and he answered viewer mail, even viewer Christmas cards. I took dictation from Jerry as he personally responded to each and every letter or card from viewers. (The briefest response to viewers was from investigative reporter Maury Green. He would receive long, sometimes as many as ten pages, viewer rants about a piece he did. He always gave the same reply: "Dear Sir or Madam, You may be right. Sincerely, Maury Green.") Jerry was solid at anchoring hard news and an expert at ad-libbing with sports and weather reporters. He arrived at the station each day at 4:30 p.m. for rehearsal of the back half of the broadcast.

It was then, as it is now, subject to change for breaking news, but at that time, the daily routine was to rehearse Jerry with weatherman Bill Keene and sportscaster Gil Stratton, whose segments ran in the back half of *The Big News*.

Weatherman Bill Keene was much beloved by Southern Californians, so much so that when he was fired because station consultants deemed LA's viewers didn't care about weather reports and KNXT didn't need a weathercaster, viewers protested, and Channel 2's ratings dropped. Keene had cornball jokes. "Hot today, chili tomorrow" was one. He talked on the air about predicting the weather based on conversations he had with KNXT's janitorial staff member Kenner Brown. Kenner had bunions, and if Kenner's bunions bothered her, then she said it was going to rain.

Sportscaster Gil Stratton lived sports. Gil's daily sports reports were a significant part of *The Big News*'s success. He started his segment saying, "Time to call 'em as I see 'em." Earlier in his career, he'd been an actor in major films and was one of the stars of *Stalag 17*.

Reporter Paul Udell would fill in as anchor during Dunphy's vacations. Paul had local contacts and was ahead of the competition on investigative stories. Udell was handsome. One interview subject referred to him as a "blue-eyed devil" during a live shot. He had a hard time living that down in the newsroom. Our competition at Channel 4 management was nervous about their own ratings should Udell become anchor of the 11:00 p.m. news if Dunphy ever left, but they had twenty-two-year-old Tom Brokaw as a member of their reporting staff and promoted him to anchor, boosting his career.

Ralph Story gave viewers a daily segment called "Human Predicament." No one in LA had a delivery like Ralph. He made you feel the event he talked about. He had two solid writers, Nate Kaplan and Bill O'Hallaren, and Ralph would write pieces as well.

No matter the writer, it was Ralph's heartfelt delivery that was key. He left *The Big News* to join KNXT's program department where a program was being developed, *Ralph Story's Los Angeles*, that became one of the most successful programs in Los Angeles television history.

Big News Team on KNXT Election set, 1964

Big News Team reunion, L to R, Ralph Story, Bill Keene, Ruth
Ashton Taylor, myself, Jerry Dunphy, Gil Stratton and Joseph Benti

Chapter 24

Behind the Scenes of *The Big News*

Everyone at the station went to Nurse Angie who, while not part of the news team, was a psychological sounding board for all. Angie always made time for you in her nurse's office. If your visit was medical, then she took care of you. If it was just to sound off, then she listened. And she was known for her advice.

When the KNXT business manager, Berte Hackett, became concerned about our *Big News* team crossing Gower Street to get to the Naples between the 6:00 p.m. and 11:00 p.m. news broadcasts, she had a fence installed with a one-way gate, facing Naples. That didn't stop *The Big News* team. Not wanting to walk down the street to a signal at Sunset and Gower, they invented a way to climb over the fence back into CBS's parking lot just in time to make the 11:00 p.m. broadcast. The business manager had more fencing added to the top of the gate. Still not defeated, Keene and Stratton climbed the fence one night, Keene tearing his pants. Always pros, they still made it on time for their slot in the broadcast.

Office administrator Bette Penny had been the sole female in the news department for several years. She was an energetic, vivacious redhead who told me her mother was a big fan of actress Bette

Davis and took young Bette to see all of Davis's films. When I first joined the newsroom, Bette was not what I would term welcoming. I had the feeling she didn't like me, but I didn't know why. One afternoon, Bette approached me and asked if I would like to go for a drink. It turned out to be a breakthrough in our relationship. She said she initially resented me because I came from Television City and had replaced a woman she was particularly fond of named Melinda Cotton. The position I filled was vacant after Melinda left to join the staff of *Ralph Story's Los Angeles*. Bette and I talked about her expectations of me and what I needed to do to fulfill the job requirements. The discussion helped me from being hindered by my fear of doing something wrong. Bette and I became good friends and when I went on trips she would throw "Bon Voyage" parties for me and invite the news staff to her home.

Our entertainment reporter, David Sheehan, knew about Bette Penny's admiration for actress Bette Davis. David was going to cover the American Film Institute's red carpet event at the Beverly Hilton honoring Davis's long career. He said he wanted to arrange for Bette Penny to attend the event and asked if I would accompany her, saying he didn't think she would attend alone. I was thrilled. Bette and I bought gowns and got our hair styled. We had David's tickets and were seated two tables over from Bette Davis. She entered the ballroom escorted on the arms of actress Natalie Wood and her husband, actor Robert Wagner. Bette and I commented we'd never seen a more glamorous threesome. There were a lot of celebrities in attendance that night. The most handsome couple had to be actress Angie Dickinson and actor David Janssen, star of the popular television show *The Fugitive*, dating and looking very much in love. At the close of Bette Davis's acceptance speech, she thanked everyone and said she wanted to use her favorite line from her movies: "I'd like to kiss you, but I just washed my hair."

Chapter 25

Discovering New Talent: Producing Auditions

My administrative position evolved into one with more respon-sibility, where I also produced talent auditions for the sta-tion. One day, I had a phone call from the news director at a station in Fresno, California. He said there was a radio newsman named Patrick Emory from KFWB in Los Angeles whom he was inter-ested in and asked if I would call him and produce an in-studio cam-era audition with Emory reading news copy; it would save having Emory come up to Fresno, he said. I was astonished when Pat Emory showed up at the studio; he was handsome in a Rock Hudson sort of way. The camera loved him, and as we were in the studio taping, there happened to be a tour group from a local school looking at the monitors. The group, who thought Emory was actually live on-air, began asking who he was. I brought his audition tape to the news director and suggested he take a look at it before sending it off to Fresno. He agreed Emory was very good and chose him as KNXT's new anchorman, despite Emory never having actually applied for a job as an anchor at Channel 2. The news director in Fresno was not happy when hearing this news..

Jim Mitchell was a longtime local radio news reporter. I had listened to him and admired his work and had noticed other reporters, including ours, making remarks such as "Check Mitchell. He's always on scene of the story before anyone else has the facts." I called Jim and asked to meet him. He was short and scruffy, and everything about him spoke of his knowledge of Los Angeles crime stories and his love of covering news. I talked to our news director and suggested Mitchell as someone he should meet. They did, and the next morning, the news director told me, "You're absolutely right." He hired Jim Mitchell, who made the transition from radio to television news with no problem. He won several journalism awards for investigative news coverage.

Often, the news director had no interest in the reporter, sportscaster, or whomever; it was simply a way of going through the motions and then rejecting the applicant. Once, there was a lovely young lady who came in for an audition. I asked for her resume; she didn't know what that was. She said she'd never done any work in television news. Her explanation for coming in was that she sold ice cream at Thrifty Drugs, had met the station's general manager and apparently caught his eye, and he said she ought to be on television. I talked to the news director and said it was a waste of studio time and crew production. I told her politely that there were currently no openings.

Some candidates you would think could be great on-air were surprisingly bad. One was Mark Harmon, who was looking into the possibility of following his father's footsteps into sports reporting. Dad Tom Harmon was hugely popular and successful in the position. Mark, who was handsome and personable, did not prove to be ready for an on-air spot. Of course, he later went into acting, and the rest is history. I saw Mark several years later when he came into the station to do an interview to promote a movie in which he was starring.

We talked about his sports audition, and he said he was thankful he didn't get the job because his career in film and TV had turned out to be the better avenue for him. He's a lovely guy who deserves to star in the number one show in ratings: *NCIS*.

Dodgers' player Don Sutton also auditioned for a television sportscasting job. While I was producing his audition, I mentioned my father was a big fan. When the audition was finished, Sutton thanked me and left the station. An hour later, he returned and handed me an autographed photo to give to my dad. The next time I saw Don Sutton was at our sportscaster Jim Hill's wedding. Hill's ushers, groomsmen, and attendees included many athletes. Upon arrival at the door of the church, many familiar faces met me. Out of the group stepped Don Sutton, always a first-class guy, who announced to the others he would be the one escorting me to my seat.

Everyone wanted to work at KNXT Channel 2 News. The CBS-owned-and-operated television news station in Los Angeles was the premier place to work and the goal of reporters and anchors hoping to be on the air at the best station in the country. I know because it was my job to produce the on-air talent auditions: to screen videotapes submitted from reporters and/or their talent agent managers. In viewing the tapes, if I spotted someone with potential, then I would bring the tape to the attention of my news director boss; otherwise, I would return the video with a rejection letter.

Chapter 26

Bob Long: The Consummate Broadcast Journalist

There was no one in the news business more intelligent, respected, or capable than Bob Long. Adding to that, he possessed the best sense of humor of anyone on the planet. Long was our assignment desk manager, a title that doesn't begin to describe his capabilities. He was more responsible for Channel 2 News getting exclusives and arriving first at breaking news stories than anyone in local news coverage. He was a twenty-two-year-old ex-marine when he first arrived at Channel 2 News for an interview with assistant news director Patrick O'Reilly. He told of succeeding in getting an interview with Cuba's Fidel Castro at only fourteen years old. Castro was in Washington, DC, touring the nation's capital, and young Bob Long somehow gained access to Castro's entourage and scored that interview.

Our exclusive coverage of the shootout between the SLA (Symbionese Liberation Party) and Los Angeles police was due to Bob Long's coordination. Everyone in the country carried KNXT, Channel 2's live coverage of the shootout between the SLA and LAPD. SLA members kidnapped Patty Hearst on February 4, 1974, and were holding her hostage. Nineteen-year-old heiress Hearst was the daughter of Randolph Hearst and granddaughter of newspaper tycoon William Randolph Hearst. A tip came to the LAPD that the SLA was holed up in a house on East Fifty-Fourth in South LA and possibly had Hearst in the house. Reporters Bob Simmons and Bill Diez were live at the scene using the new minicam handheld camera, "news now" technology pioneered by CBS and KNXT. Six SLA members died during the two-hour shootout and the fire that engulfed the house. On that day, May 17 1974, KNXT's live television coverage was watched by thousands nationally and internationally, including Hearst, who was not in the house; she was in a home in Orange County with two SLA members, Bill and Emily Harris, watching our exclusive reporting of the shootout. Hearst and the Harrises were eventually captured in 1976. Her kidnapping and alliance with the SLA was offered as an example of Stockholm syndrome, the bonding of a victim with her captors while being held prisoner. She was tried and convicted of carrying out crimes with the SLA. Hearst served twenty-one months. President Jimmy Carter commuted her sentence. President Bill Clinton later pardoned her in 2001.

Bob Long left Channel 2 News after news director Bill Eames was replaced and transferred to the Washington, DC, CBS stations' division. Bob was immensely loyal to Bill and, in fact, wrote in his resignation memo that he no longer wanted to work for a company that could remove a news director with Bill's qualifications and experience to bring in someone from another city to head up the greatest news department in the country. The two had a strong business and personal relationship rare in the newsroom. Bob was the only person permitted by Bill to kiddingly refer to him as "Lefty." Bill had lost an arm in an accident as a child. Bob did not use the term in a derogatory way but with affection.

Bob Long called me "Bubbles." Walking into the newsroom, I would often hear him shout out from the assignment desk, "Bubbles, come over here. I need you to check on something for me." In 2011, we were at the House of Blues on the Sunset Strip for our Channel 2 reunion. The venue was so crowded with former and current staffers that it was a challenge to get to see and talk with everyone. I was making my way across the room when I heard a familiar voice call out, "Bubbles!" Bob Long had made the trip from Washington, DC, to attend the reunion. He wore his usual attire, a vest and bow tie. He brought that same sense of humor we all knew.

Bob Long died on August 30, 2016, at George Washington University Hospital. He was seventy-two years old.

As an aside, news director Bill Eames once implemented a directive to never use the term "ex" when referring to former presidents of the United States. (He sent a memo to news writers and producers stating the term should only be used when writing about former wives or husbands.) While I was working under Bill, Ed Joyce offered me a job as his administrative assistant at WCBS Television in New York. It was a flattering offer but would have been a lateral move career wise. Since I had just purchased my first home in Encino, and my son and his family were nearby in Mar Vista, I declined Ed's offer. I might add the East Coast weather was a factor, since I'm a native Californian and had never lived anyplace else. Ed Joyce, the news director at WCBS-TV, later became president of CBS News.

News Director Bill Eames was a family man. He directed me to make an excuse to get him out of late evening meetings and said "I'm going to be with Pat (his wife) a lot longer than I'll be with this job." Bill and Assistant News Director Al Greenstein asked me to join them for drinks at Room at the Top, a restaurant at the top of a high rise building at the corner of Sunset and Vine Street. I didn't know the purpose of the meeting and was concerned about my job. The three of us had a round of drinks when Bill said to

Al "why don't you tell Lorraine the good news." My job had been re-classified at their request, approved, and I was getting a salary increase outside my annual increase. The two were smiling like two proud papas.

Bill Eames, myself and Bob Long

Chapter 27

Dave Lopez: Complete Coverage at Its Best

My news director boss, Bob Schaefer, hired Dave Lopez. Forty-five years later, he's still reporting at the CBS station, KCBS, Channel 2 in Los Angeles. I told my many news interns who were studying journalism the best example I could show them was video of Dave Lopez's reporting. When he did a live shot on a breaking news story or reported from the scene of a press conference, you as a viewer were witnessing a complete, factual news report, and no question remained. The best news reporter in the business of covering Southern California and giving television viewers the whole story, objectively, Dave is a reporter with a wealth of news sources, who is known for his accuracy in reporting. Dave is someone other reporters seek out when arriving at a story, since he's well known for nailing the facts ahead of everyone. Our own Channel 2 news producer, Mike Daniels, who taught journalism at Loyola, told me he borrowed tapes of Dave Lopez's news reports to show to his journalism students, again an example of how to tell a story, completely and accurately, with no questions on the viewer's part after the report was finished. Dave covered major Southern California news stories: Richard Ramirez (The Night Stalker); serial killers Randy Kraft and William Bonin; missing Westlake Village doctor Robert Axelrod; and convicted kidnap murderer David Westerfield, who killed seven-year-old Danielle van Dam. Lopez reported the kidnapping of South Lake Tahoe eleven-year-old Jaycee Dugard in 1991 and her rescue eighteen years later in 2009.

Chapter 28

Political Experiences

Beginning in 1972, CBS assigned me to work at the Democratic and Republican National Conventions in July and August. In August 1972, the Republican Convention was held in Miami. It was a time of unrest due to protests against the Vietnam War. The news media was working out of trailers adjacent to the arena where the Republican Convention was taking place. Miami law enforcement and city officials had ordered placement of buses end to end in the streets surrounding the arena. It was President Richard Nixon's convention leading to his second term in office. There was some chatter among Republican delegates about Watergate, but the talk was that it was not going to amount to anything and would not influence the president's reelection. Police fired tear gas at the demonstrators, which went into the arena and surrounding area. I was wearing contact lenses and had never experienced exposure to tear gas before; it's overwhelming: difficult to breathe and painful to the eyes. As assistant bureau chief, I set up CBS stations' working space and distributed press credentials to correspondents (some stations sent their anchors as well as political reporters). The most famous incident at the convention was when performer Sammy Davis joined President

Nixon on the stage, greeting the president with a big hug, all to Nixon's astonishment. The GOP audience laughed and applauded Davis. Nixon's opponent was US Senator George McGovern of South Dakota. Nixon was reelected, but he resigned in 1974 following the Watergate investigation.

At the Miami Republican National Convention, 1972

From July 12–15, 1976, I was assigned to work at the Democratic National Convention, held in New York City's Madison Square Garden. A history-making convention, it was the first in New York since the 103-ballot 1924 convention. Lindy Boggs, Louisiana congresswoman, was the first woman to preside over a national political convention. Texas Congresswoman Barbara Jordan, an African American, delivered the keynote address. Our Channel 2 Los Angeles correspondent was Ruth Ashton Taylor. Former Georgia Governor Jimmy Carter won the Democratic nomination for president and chose US Senator Walter Mondale of Minnesota as his vice-presidential running mate. The Carter-Mondale ticket was elected. They served from January 20, 1977, to January 20, 1981. Carter and Mondale lost the 1980 election to Ronald Reagan and George H. W. Bush.

Press Pass, 1976 Democratic National Convention

President Carter visited Channel 2 in Los Angeles twice. The first visit was during his presidency when he held a town hall meeting in one of our studios on May 17, 1977. Staffers were asked to attend to assure seats were filled. The second occasion was after he left the White House and was on a several-city book tour. Carter came into the studio for an interview. Secret service agents and his book publicist accompanied him. Several of us went to the studio to see him, myself included. I brought a *TIME* magazine "Man of the Year" issue, and the man that year was President Carter. I hoped he would sign the magazine cover. I introduced myself. Mr. Carter said he'd like to wait until he finished his interview. Forty-five minutes later, when the program was over, there were many people waiting to take photos and to have him sign their copies of his book.

He called out, "Where's Lorraine?" I came forward, and the former president signed my *TIME* magazine. He then put his arm around my shoulder and proceeded to walk around the stage with me as his tour guide. I asked him if he remembered being in this same studio for his town hall meeting years before. He said, "Lorraine, you and I are probably the only people who remember that." After our walk, President Carter stayed and posed for photos with employees, myself included. No matter how many political figures and celebrities I'd met, that memory of the former president of the United States, with his arm around my shoulder while walking and reminiscing about an event that occurred during his term as president, is special.

With President Jimmy Carter

The Republican National Convention that year was held in August at Kemper Arena in Kansas City, Missouri. Kansas City welcomed convention delegates and news media covering the day-to-day events. A city known for having the best barbecue kept restaurants open after hours so that when we finished work we could grab a brew and a bite to eat. Gerald Ford won the nomination for president but not without some competition from former California Governor Ronald Reagan. When the ballots were counted, Ford selected US Senator Bob Dole of Kansas as his vice-presidential running mate.

The 1980 Republican Convention was held at Joe Louis Arena in Detroit. I was dispatched to Chicago far before the start of the convention, since Detroit, the "Motor City," didn't have enough rental cars to fill requests from the networks. I met a woman sent from CBS's Washington bureau in Chicago, and we drove two cars to Detroit. Our CBS reporters and crews were housed at the Renaissance Hotel in Detroit, a hotel that looked exactly like LA's downtown Bonaventure Hotel. We worked long days and late hours. Restaurants in Detroit were closed; however, many restaurants in Windsor, Canada, made an exception and stayed open until the wee hours. It was a short drive through the Detroit/Windsor Tunnel into Canada.

I was on the convention floor when Ronald Reagan, former governor of California, won the nomination in 1980. I thought back to the time I was a young fan and corresponded with the then-Hollywood film actor. I remembered the time my friend Marie and I sat in the bleachers outside the Carthay Circle Theater and saw Ronald Reagan and then-wife actress Jane Wyman arrive for the premier of his film *Stallion Road*. Reagan and Wyman came over to us, said hello, and signed our autograph books. As young teenage fans, meeting Ronald Reagan was exciting and emotional for us. I had seen Reagan once again when he was governor of California and came to KNXT Channel 2 for a news interview. He selected former CIA director George H. W. Bush of Texas as his vice-presidential running mate. They went on to win the election and the White House.

I worked in New York at Madison Square Garden once again for the 1980 Democratic Convention. Another four years saw the return of Jimmy Carter and Walter Mondale. Walter Cronkite anchored our

CBS News coverage, with correspondents Roger Mudd, Dan Rather, Bob Schieffer, Mike Wallace, and Ed Bradley. Cronkite was known nationally as the most trusted man in America. In my view, he was the consummate journalist, and it was an honor to know him and work with him. Dan Rather and I went way back; he was a close friend of Bill Eames, my news director boss at Channel 2 News. Ed Bradley and I became friends and remained so over the years. Schieffer, Mudd, and Wallace were three of the best correspondents in television news as well as some of the nicest people in the business. Our Channel 2 News correspondent from Los Angeles, Bill Stout, was a longtime friend of Walter Cronkite's. At the close of the convention and sign-off of CBS's television coverage, Stout did an interview with Walter in the broadcast booth above the convention floor. Stout's opening question to Cronkite, who had been anchoring CBS's four-day convention coverage, was "Walter, how's your ass?"

With CBS anchor Dan Rather

Channel 2 News subscribed to Mervin Field's exclusive Field Poll, a well-known political poll-gathering source with results airing exclusively on our news. Political commentators at other networks offered exclusive reports on our Field Poll after they aired on Channel 2 News. But that exclusivity didn't stop other reporters from trying to learn the poll results before we aired them. Such was the case with ABC News's Sam Donaldson. I have to say I admired his ingenuity. My news director boss and I were the only ones at the station who saw the poll results before air. I got a phone call from Sam Donaldson, who hurriedly said, "These are the poll numbers I have from the Field Poll. Do these numbers correspond with yours?"

He began to read the supposed numbers he had, hoping I would say, "Oh no, let me correct those for you." Instead, I replied, "Good try, Sam, but no. I'm not sharing the Field Poll results with you."

And then he said, "Well, OK. It was nice talking with you."

I was privileged to witness political history over many years covering both parties' conventions. I never dreamed I would witness my country's more recent history-making event; that is, the daughter of a living US president, who grew up in the White House, introducing her mother at the Democratic Convention in Philadelphia—her mother who is the first woman nominated from a major party for president of the United States. Due to live television, I was able to witness this history with my grandchildren.

Over the years, I corresponded with many political figures. In 1968, I wrote a note to Nelson Rockefeller in which I expressed my hope that he would change his mind about running for president on the Republican ticket. I received a letter dated April 8, 1968, from the New York governor in response to my note. It reads:

While I have not felt that it was in the interest of the party or the country for me to become an active candidate campaigning for the nomination, especially in the primaries, I have tried to make it clear that I will not shirk any responsibility that should be mine in this time of deepening crisis.

Thus, I have not removed myself from consideration for the Republican presidential nomination. As I have said, I will be speaking out on the issues and I will stand ready to answer any true and meaningful call from the Republican Party to serve it and the nation. My appreciation for your encouragement.

Sincerely,

Nelson Rockefeller

Rockefeller was considered a progressive moderate of the Republican party. He served as New York governor from 1959 to 1973. President Gerald Ford appointed him vice president of the United States in 1974. Ford, who was President Nixon's vice president, became president following Nixon's resignation over Watergate. Ford then selected Rockefeller as his vice president, only the second time a vice president was appointed under provisions of the Twenty-Fifth Amendment. Rockefeller did not join the 1976 ticket with Ford. Ford selected Senator Bob Dole of Kansas as his running mate. Rockefeller retired from politics. He died January 26, 1979.

Late one evening, I was home in Encino, California, when my telephone rang. When I answered, a woman's voice said, "I hope I'm not too late with this." It was First Lady Barbara Bush calling about a letter I had written. Knowing of her interest in and support of education, I had written her several weeks earlier about the son of a friend. David, a hearing-impaired young man, had excelled in school and was graduating from high school with honors. David always called me his honorary aunt. He was special to me, so I had written Mrs. Bush in the hope she would write a letter congratulating him on his accomplishment. Indeed, she did. She apologized for not getting the letter in the mail sooner. I was amazed and admittedly tongue-tied realizing I was speaking directly with the first lady, who had placed the call herself. I hold all of our first ladies in high esteem. I found Mrs. Bush to be warm and down to earth. I thanked her for her thoughtfulness. Shortly after the call, David received a congratulatory handwritten letter from Barbara Bush. It's framed and on display in his home.

Chapter 29

Mary Tyler Moore

I've been asked many times whether *The Mary Tyler Moore Show* was based on our KNXT newsroom. The answer is yes, to some extent. Our Channel 2 business manager, Alberta "Berte" Hackett, was Mary Tyler Moore's aunt; Berte and Mary's father were sister and brother. Before the show started production, producers James L. Brooks and Allan Burns asked my boss, Bill Eames, if they and members of the cast, along with production designers, could visit our newsroom. In they came, and what fun it was having them around. Ted Knight, who played hilarious anchorman Ted Baxter on the show, came over to my desk and whispered to me that he'd like to sit in the news director's office and put his feet up on the desk. Bill Eames was out of the office, so, yes, I took Ted in. He picked up a sign on the desk that said "News Director," held it up, and asked me to pretend I was taking dictation from him. A CBS publicist was accompanying Ted, and he asked the photographer to come in and take pictures of the two of us. He was such a charming, funny man who helped to make *The Mary Tyler Moore Show* an immediate hit. I've been asked if Ted Knight based his portrayal of anchorman Ted Baxter on our anchor Jerry Dunphy. I think the character was a composite of KTLA's longtime anchor George Putnam and Jerry, but mainly Baxter was an original role that Knight and the show's writers created to perfection. Gavin McLeod, who played writer Murray Slaughter, and Valerie Harper, who played Mary's friend Rhoda Morgenstern, also visited our newsroom. Was Ed Asner's character, news director Lou Grant, based on anyone I know? Maybe. There was a little of the captain, Pete Noyes, who was an original and could never be duplicated. He ran the newsroom and *The Big News*, and no one stepped out of line. He was the reason *The Big News* team was such a success. And there was my news director boss, Grant Holcomb, who was good friends with Mary's aunt Berte. And of course, the name Lou "Grant," or as Mary would say, "Mr. Grant."

Chapter 30

Blue Book Policy: CBS Standards and Practices

Each member of the news staff attended news policy meetings to go over, one by one, the dos and don'ts of the Blue Book, CBS's policy and standards book. Standards and practices news policy was that no staging was to take place when covering a news story. Sometimes, the no-staging policy became a little outrageous. Reporter Jim Brown and crew were covering the opening of a new ride at Disneyland, and Brown decided to enhance the piece by having a group of station employees gather and sing the Disney theme M-I-C-K-E-Y spelling out M-O-U-S-E to the music and lay sound over his video. It was an innocent idea, but not really, according to the policy masters. When another LA station's crew saw Jim Brown's piece on the air, they filed a protest, saying they covered the same event, and there was no music and singing; therefore, it was deemed staging. Jim Brown was suspended for a few days but remained at the station for many years as one of our best reporters. Another example of staging was when a reporter went to cover an event where a bubble machine was in use; however, by the time Channel 2's reporter arrived on the scene, the machine had been turned off.

She asked the owner of the property to turn the machine back on for her piece. Again, the news policy standards folks deemed this staging.

There was another strict policy at the station and throughout CBS: no sexual harassment would be tolerated. Every manager had a copy of the Blue Book stating the rules. There were periodic mandatory policy meetings held in the audience studio. Managers were instructed about what procedures to take should someone working in their department come to them about a sexual harassment incident. If the department manager failed to act, and the harassment escalated and was reported to company management, then the fallout would be on the manager as well as the perpetrator because the manager had failed to act.

I had male and female student interns from various universities working for class credit in my news research department. Because they were young and vulnerable, they tended to be approached by those in power. And because they were new at the station, they didn't know how to respond, fearful they might lose their internship if they made any waves. It wasn't only female interns who experienced harassment; male interns came to me as well. One young man asked me if he was expected to go to dinner with a male reporter who asked him out the second day he was at the station and repeatedly asked him out to dinner during his first week. I told him firmly no. The reporter was known in the news department for his pressure on young male news associates. I told my intern I would handle the situation, and he was not required to go out with anyone, no matter how much pressure they put on him. I called the reporter in for a talk. He'd been at the station awhile, was really popular with viewers, and was thought of in the LA community as an all-around nice guy. I explained I'd had a complaint and told him as a manager I was required to report his actions to the general manager of the station unless he agreed to cease his behavior. That talk resulted in the end of his actions. Fortunately, I never needed to go to the general manager and was able to keep the situation from escalating.

One female intern complained to me that no matter where she went—the coffee machine in the lunchroom, the park where she rode her bike during lunch, or elsewhere—a certain man kept looming and asking her out, intimidating her. Again, I told her just because he was a person in a powerful position, she was under no obligation to go out with him. I called him in for a meeting and told him that if he persisted in harassing her, then I would need to go to the general manager. I wanted to give him the opportunity to cease his behavior. The harassment stopped. What the station didn't want was a lawsuit filed by the parents of a student intern over a situation we could remedy.

I recall showing a new female intern the control room. When we entered the booth one of the male techs turned to us and pointing to his lap gesturing for her to sit and said to the intern "put it here baby."

Since I began to write this book, I was told by former women coworkers in news and in other departments at the station that they experienced sexual harassment. Because of the Blue Book policy, CBS would not tolerate any type of harassment. However, it was suggested to these women that they "should try to just get along."

I, too, experienced unwanted touching. Early in my days in the KNXT newsroom, before the Blue Book policy, there was a gruff cameraman who would see me walking across the room, catch up with me, and put his hand down to flip my skirt up in front of everyone in the newsroom. It was embarrassing, and I tried to dodge him. The worst humiliation he caused, however, was at a Southern California journalism awards dinner. He was seated at a table with his wife. I walked by their table, and he reached out and flipped my skirt up in front of her and anyone within view. What could I do? I avoided him and gave him icy stares. Though management witnessed and was aware of his transgressions, he never faced any repercussions and eventually left the station for another job.

Chapter 31

Affairs and Indiscretions

There were many affairs at Channel 2; some between married news anchors were publicized in local newspapers. There were also late-night calls to the news assignment desk from partners or spouses asking whether the editor knew the whereabouts of someone who hadn't come home. One station executive told his wife he had late-night "strike training." It was also common practice for people to hook up at seminars away from the station. Spouses were not invited; the seminars were designed to conduct news department business such as exchanging sweeps ideas and how to build ratings, along with how to publicize sweeps campaigns. Men known in the community as family men devoted to their wives and families were tempted to stray. Often, their indiscretions made the press.

During my early years at Channel 2 News, I often went to the station lobby to talk to young women who came in to try to see an anchorman they had become acquainted with; the women were younger than the anchors' daughters. Station management told me to get rid of them. In other words, to make the situation go away. One woman wrote letters to an anchor while parked in her car outside the building on El Centro and then hand-carried them to the guard and asked him to deliver them.

In one instance, I learned from a female reporter that my former news director boss told her he thought I had opened his office door and seen him engaged with a woman staffer. But it wasn't me—one of my jobs as his assistant was to keep staffers from opening his office door. The reporter and I had a good laugh since, had I known I supposedly had this knowledge, I could have used it to my advantage. I probably had job security for a reason I didn't know about.

I considered whether to make this a tell-all book, but the decision was no. The subjects may be gone, but they left behind families who could be hurt.

Chapter 32

Change: For Better or Worse

Every so often, the station brought in consulting firms to study the newsroom. They were not hired to file reports saying everything was fine and that there was no change necessary, but their suggestions for improvements were more often misses than hits. In the evaluation of *The Big News*, the general manager and news director took their opinion seriously. Consultants decided anchor Jerry Dunphy was finished in the LA market and also that LA viewers didn't care about the weather, so longtime beloved weatherman Bill Keene was let go as well. The story of Dunphy leaving has made the rounds for years; it's all true. Channel 2's general manager, Russ Barry, called KABC's general manager, John Severino, and asked, "If I let Jerry Dunphy go, you won't hire him will you?" Severino said no. Shortly thereafter, Jerry was out. The rest is history. Severino did indeed hire him. He paired Jerry with an attractive younger woman coanchor. KABC's ratings shot up and beat *The Big News*.

Later, Russ and Severino were playing tennis, and Russ asked about their conversation in which Severino said he would never hire Dunphy. Severino responded, "I lied." Although Jerry Dunphy left KNXT he stayed loyal to those he'd worked with so many years.

I remember the night Jerry came by the station and picked up Carole Gardner and myself in his silver blue Rolls (a car given him by KABC's management when he joined that station). Jerry drove Carole and I to his favorite Beverly Hills restaurant, Café Swiss, where he had the chef prepare a special dinner for us. Jerry loved music and was composing songs with his son-in-law, Mike Curb. In 1983 I received a phone call from Jerry. He said he was a patient at Hollywood Presbyterian Hospital, and was recovering from gunshot wounds received in a robbery attempt ambush outside KABC's parking lot. I went to visit Jerry in the hospital. Jerry returned to anchor at KCBS in 1995, and left to anchor at KCAL-TV Channel 9 two years later. Jerry died of a heart attack May 20, 2002. I attended his funeral at Saint Cyril's Church in Encino.

Once, Channel 2 hired a husband-and-wife team of psychological consultants to work with our female and male coanchor team, who hated each other and didn't speak to each other off-air. Ironically, the consultants themselves were going through a divorce and didn't speak to each other outside the business sessions they were paid to conduct. There were consultants who instructed me to open and close the blinds in the news director's office periodically during the day so that the staff wouldn't think there was something secretive taking place inside his office, which had a large glass window looking out at the newsroom. I was ridiculously asked to open and close those blinds whether there was anyone in the office or not. Psychology 101 the psychologists laughingly told me.

And then there was the consultant's suggestion we broadcast live from the newsroom. Anchors and reporters would walk around, and some sat not at their desks but on top of them. Distraction and noise reigned. Staffers would forget we were live; one female news associate was seen giving one of our male news writers a neck rub on the air. It wasn't long before the broadcast was moved back to the studio. This same consulting team had the station staff complete questionnaires about management. A meeting was held with all of us in attendance to discuss the questionnaire results. One of the results announced was that the current general manager was "a bad GM because he learned from other bad GMs." He was present and made no comment.

Chapter 33

That Firing Friday

The *Los Angeles Times* ran an article about the Friday firings, twenty-two discharges in one day. A new team of GMs and news directors—the Saint Louis mob, or so they were nicknamed—arrived in 1976 and initiated the discharge. That day, I had the unfortunate duty of locating each person the news director wanted to see and bringing him or her to his office. The mass dismissal at KNXT in June 1976 included anchors Patrick Emory and Sandy Hill; reporters Ciji Ware, Greg Risch, Jim Murphy, Bob Navarro, Bob Simmons, and Bill Applegate; sportscaster Tom Kelly; and news writers Michele Willens, Mike Bloebaum, and Mark Litke. In anchorwoman Sandy Hill's case, the general manager asked that I escort her to his office after she finished anchoring the broadcast, collect her purse from her desk, and bring it to his office. In other words, he did not want her to go to the newsroom; he planned to have her exit the building from a door outside his office that led to Sunset Boulevard. Sandy was furious with me but later forgave me and said she understood the position I'd been in. One of those fired, Bill Applegate, got the last laugh. He said he'd be back and returned as general manager from 1993 to 1996.

Chapter 34

"We Got Connie"

I first met anchors Jess Marlow and John Schubeck at KNBC, Channel 4, our chief competition, when I was invited by the director of their *News at Eleven* to visit their set. Jess was the nicest, kindest man and offered to take me on a personal tour of the newsroom. Afterward, he escorted me in to see Johnny Carson's set, which was adjacent to the news set, and he introduced me to Carson. John Schubeck was even handsomer than he appeared on air. He had aqua-blue eyes and loads of appeal. He was cordial in greeting me. Little did I know, I would be working with both Jess and John a few years later when they left Channel 4 to join our KNXT, Channel 2 News.

I was in New York working once again at a political convention when I received a call from news director Bob Schaefer in Los Angeles. His words said it all: "We got Connie." He and general manager Chris Desmond had been attempting to hire newswoman Connie Chung. Her arrival at KNXT raised the morale of the newsroom, and Southern California viewers loved her. Our news ratings went up, particularly when Connie was teamed with Jess Marlow. I can remember a celebratory party in the newsroom after the news broadcast when Connie and Jess climbed on the anchor desk and did a tap dance together.

Make-up artist Joanna Charles, Connie Chung and myself

Sometime later, a different news management decided to try out a two-woman anchor team: Connie Chung and Marcia Brandwynne. Viewers didn't take to Marcia at first, although she quickly grew on them and won their approval. The station, however, didn't give the team time to work, and they let Marcia go. The manner in which it was done was without regard for her feelings. Marcia arrived for work, and upon driving through the artists' entrance gate at Columbia Square, she was told not to get out of her car. The news director fired her in the parking lot. Her release was picked up by the newspapers and was a topic of talk radio. Channel 2 underestimated viewer response: they were furious and phoned and wrote angry letters to the station, coming to Marcia's defense. She was soon picked up by another station that recognized her popularity with the LA audience.

Chapter 35

New Direction

Each new general manager worked with two news directors—the one in the position upon his arrival, and the replacement he inevitably brought in. In any case, a news director was brought on board, not from within but from another city. Next, the same old formula was trotted out: replace the anchors and/or replace the set. What the powers that be never seemed to understand was a news program must contain two elements: first and foremost, it has to tell the viewer what's going on, and second, it should tell some things a viewer should know, even though the viewer may have no curiosity about them. It should have interesting presentations, first-rate production techniques, and complete coverage. Nothing was going to be a quick fix. The new news director, always a male, would hold a staff meeting to introduce himself, and it was pretty much the same talk we'd heard before: "I'm here to bring us together. I'm open to suggestions," and "My door is always open." Which, of course, it never was. I know. It was part of my job to keep certain people out of his office. We had one news director who actually hid in the closet in his office. It was very tiny, with no light, and barely enough room to stand and close the door because there was a small refrigerator inside. Sometimes I would call him, and then think maybe he went out the outer door since there were two exits, one by my desk and the other directly to the hallway on the other side of the office. The situation provided the staff with a lot of laughs.

Each new management shift brought an evaluation of and then changes to news sets and/or news broadcast anchors. Channel 2's viewers liked consistency and wrote and phoned the station when sets or anchors changed, but the changes were numerous. One change in a news set even received negative comments such as "What was it before it fell?"

With expansions occurring, anchor changes soon followed, with new and improved promotional campaigns. Channel 2 News ran a campaign in the *LA Times* the week of October 30, 1977: "What They Uncover Today, the Others Report Tomorrow." A photo of anchors Connie Chung and Maury Povich was featured. (Connie and Maury met at the station, began dating, and later married.) The ad also featured an upcoming segment airing November 6, 1977: "Does This Man Have a Future in Politics?" reported by Connie Chung. The man in question was Jerry Brown, then serving his first term as the governor of California. He did indeed have a future in politics. In 2011, he was inaugurated to be California's governor again and currently holds the position.

In 1978, the promotional campaign read "Introducing the Country's First 2½ Hour TV News" from four thirty to five with Mike Parker, Ralph Story, Steve Edwards, Jim Hill, and Bill Stout; five to six with Joseph Benti, Linda Douglass, Brent Musberger, Steve Edwards, and David Sheehan; and six to seven with Connie Chung, Mike Parker, Steve Edwards, Brent Musberger, Ralph Story, and Bill Stout. In May 1978, the station ran a campaign: "Story, Brandwynne, Chung and Musburger Move KNXT News Up!"

Governor Jerry Brown, myself and Ruth Ashton Taylor

With sportscaster Jim Hill

L to R, Linda Douglass, Johnathan Rodgers, Nancy Jacoby, Jay
Feldman, Karl Fleming, Pat O'Brien, Dave Corvo and Tammy Taylor

L to R, Dave Lopez, Phil Ronney, Bob Navarro, Jeff Wald, Carole Gardner, Joanna Charles, Bob Long, Patty Ecker, Bill Applegate, David Sheehan, myself, Joseph Benti and Nancy Jacoby

Two notables are Brent Musberger, sports reporter, who had moved up the ranks into an anchor spot, and reporter Bill Stout, who could be considered the conscience of Los Angeles television. Bill enjoyed reporting on the hypocrites, as he called them, in government. He did a daily "Perspective" piece and then a monthly feature called "Stout's Turkeys." I provided him with daily research and kept a file of "Turkeys": news articles I saved about various politicians' or local and national figures' shenanigans. Bill and I would go over these at the end of the month, and Bill would select the ones to be awarded a "Turkey" in his "Perspective" piece. Local officials dreaded those daily Stout "Perspectives" and especially disliked being singled out by Stout for a Turkey of the Month Award. It was Bill Stout who introduced me to the Moscow Mule. He took me to lunch at the Cock n Bull Restaurant on the Sunset Strip. The famous Moscow Mule drink originated at the British style pub located at 9170 Sunset Boulevard. The drink was a combination of vodka, ginger beer, and a lemon wedge and served in a chilled copper mug. I hadn't seen the Moscow Mule listed on menus for years until recently when I was vacationing in Florida and went with friends to the Red Bar at Grayton Beach.

Lunch at the Cock 'n Bull, L to R, Bob Long, Warren Olney, Peggy Stout, Bill Eames, myself, Rubin Green, and Bill Stout

Local news was followed by the CBS Evening News anchored by Walter Cronkite at 7:00 p.m. Our 11:00 p.m. campaign read: "11 PM News. Tomorrow's News Tonight." It offered fresh new stories, not a rehash of earlier news.

Chapter 36

Van Sauter: A Positive Arrival

In 1977, a luncheon to honor CBS employees with twenty-year tenure was held at the Beverly Wilshire Hotel in Beverly Hills. Ruth Ashton Taylor and I received special invitations. The new incoming general manager, Van Gordon Sauter, from Chicago, escorted us. I knew Van from the 1972 Republican Convention in Miami, where we shared a trailer work space/office; he was head of WBBM Chicago Radio at that time. Bob Daly, executive vice president of CBS Network, handed out the awards. In presenting mine, Mr. Daly said to the audience, "I understand Lorraine is really the person who runs the newsroom. However, if that were true, it wouldn't be in the terrible shape it's in." (He was referring to Channel 2 News's low ratings and low morale.) I have an audiotape of that luncheon ceremony and am touched by Bob Daly's remarks.

Van, who always called me "Lady," remembered me from our stint in Miami covering the Republican National Convention. He was nonconventional, living on a boat in Marina del Rey rather than buying a traditional home. He had an open and friendly manner and a casual but distinctive appearance. It wasn't unusual to see Van walking the hallway to his office wearing open-toed sandals, his dark beard flowing, followed by his black lab. He was decidedly impromptu. When I answered my office phone I heard, "Lady, come on. We're going to lunch." What followed was a ride in his Jeep with his secretary, Cynthia Park, and our publicist, Phyllis Kirk Bush. Prior to joining KNXT, Phyllis had been a leading actress in films, among them the classic House of Wax., and was very theatrical. Although she intimidated a lot of people, she was really a sweetheart when you got to know her. She called everyone, male and female, "Dahling." Off we drove to the trendy Santa Monica restaurant Michael's.

Van Sauter brought in my next two news director bosses, both from WBBM Chicago: Jay Feldman, followed by Johnathan Rodgers, our first African American news director. Johnathan came to KNXT, Channel 2 News by way of stints at *Sports Illustrated* and *Newsweek* magazines, followed by jobs as executive news producer and news director at WBBM-TV (also owned and operated by CBS) in Chicago. He set a tone and vision for the newsroom and was respected by all. He once told me that, as his personal secretary, he welcomed my input, since I had held the job for so many years and had seen numerous news directors come and go. And he added, "You are the only one who remembers how to spell my name."

Steve Cohen, News Director at WCBS-TV in New York, was named our new News Director at KCBS, Channel 2, Los Angeles, in 1982. I'd heard from friends at CBS New York that Cohen had gone through three secretaries during his short stint as News Director. It was no surprise that after I'd worked as his secretary for six months he called me into his office for a chat. Cohen said it was time I moved into a management position in the News Department and he was naming me Director of News Research, an executive position with a considerable salary increase. He complimented me in that he said he wanted an aggressive News Research Department and I was the person to head it. He assigned me to go to CBS Network News in New York to learn what resources were used at that news research department and to create the same at our west coast news operation. I did. Channel 2's research office grew, a wall was knocked down to expand, I added computers, Steve Cohen left Channel 2 and was followed by a long succession of news directors. I remained Director of News Research until my retirement from Channel 2, KCBS, in 1995.

Chapter 37

Channel 2's Secret Weapon

W hen I was promoted from secretary/news administrator of the news director to director of news research in 1982, my boss sent me to CBS News in New York to see how the network's vast news library was set up. It had newspapers on file from all over the country. My own office in LA included a large news research library, and modeling after New York, I set up files of local newspapers such as the *Herald-Examiner*, *Daily News*, *LA Times*, the trades (*Variety* and *Hollywood Reporter*), and magazines including *Time*, *Newsweek*, *People*, and *Sports Illustrated*, and multiple reference books. At that time, Facts on File was a good resource. Our news graphics department called on me for photos they could use to accompany news stories on-air, giving credit to the publication the picture came from. As research director, I was to see the assignment desk had complete, up-to-date background on breaking or ongoing stories. I kept research files that included contacts' phone numbers, dates on which we'd done earlier stories, and sources in the case of ongoing crime stories. Our reporters came to my office for research as soon as they got their assignments. On breaking news stories I would bring research to the newsroom or very often run with it to the parking lot where I met with the reporter and crew.

With Los Angeles Police Chief Daryl Gates

Later, when computers became available, I added one. I had to be able to locate stories in an instant. I set up my computer so that I could find a crime story by one word, if need be. For example, there was a local shooting where the bullet went through a window and struck and killed a young boy who was sitting at the kitchen table drinking a glass of milk. I set up my locator so that, months later, I was able to find the story by one word: milk. No one in the newsroom could remember the child's name or any detail of the story to be able to find it. But I sat down at my computer and typed in that one word. Of course, it brought up other stories about milk prices and the like, but then it brought up the sad story of the shooting of the little boy.

I'd like to say now what amazing young people my news interns over the years were, and I'm proud of each and every one. I see them anchoring or reporting at stations across the country and on cable stations FOX and CNN. One of my interns, Michele Tuzzee, is anchoring at the ABC station in Los Angeles, along with Liz Claman at FOX, Alex Witt at MSNBC, and Jason Carroll at CNN. I'm still in touch with many of them.

In my position as director of news research, it wasn't long before the news staff started calling me Rona Research. The name stuck. In February 1988, the *Los Angeles Times* did a cover story on Channel 2. Accompanying the feature was a photo of me at my desk with the headline: "Lorraine Hillman is Channel 2's Secret Weapon." My research reputation was well known at LA's other television news departments. Reporters who had moved on to other stations from Channel 2 knew what research I had available, and they weren't finding such help elsewhere. I had several requests for help from LA assignment desk reporters, and then the word seemed to spread around the country. Still, of course, I helped our own CBS News network assignment desk and correspondents first. One of our Channel 2 News producers, whose reporter wife worked for the competition, offered to pay me to give her my "research packets," which detailed the history of earthquakes or plane crashes, saying she was caught off guard on a breaking news earthquake story when reporting out in the field. I turned down his proposal.

Calls for research help sometimes came from surprising places. It was after six one evening when I received a call from my first student intern, Greg Slotta. We'd stayed in touch awhile, and I knew he'd gone to work in Washington, DC, as an aide to Secretary of State James Baker. They were driving to a location in DC where Baker was scheduled to deliver a speech. Greg said he was hoping I could help with a question about a historical fact in the secretary's speech. He didn't know if I was still at Channel 2 and was happy he could reach me. It was after 9:00 p.m. in DC, and nothing was open where he could get research. I was glad to help; anything I could do to keep a government official from making a mistake, I thought. And I was doing it for Greg. It was a pleasure to connect with him again and to learn of the high position he held.

My reputation as a know-it-all researcher brought me one offer I *could* refuse. A writer approached me from a nationally published tabloid who suggested his boss would pay me under the table for tips on stories I was working on for Channel 2 News. I gave him an immediate reply: NO.

When I retired from KCBS, Channel 2 News (KNXT, Channel 2 officially became KCBS on April 2, 1984) and before I joined ABC News, several people, including my former boss at KCBS, suggested that I open my own research business. I thought about what that venture would entail—it would have required my opening an office and hiring messengers to bring research material to reporters at all Los Angeles television stations. While I never seriously considered doing it, it was flattering because I received many calls at home from the station I left and from many other LA stations requesting my research services.

Chapter 38

Rosalva's Surprise

My research office was across from the green room, a kind of holding area where movie, television, and stage performers visiting Channel 2 for interviews would sit and relax until it was time for their live or taped interview. One day, Donny Osmond—yes, that Donny, from *Donny and Marie*—was in the green room. He was appearing in the musical *Joseph and the Amazing Technicolor Dreamcoat* at the Pantages Theatre in Hollywood and was at Channel 2 News to promote his show. I started getting interoffice phone calls from Rosalva Skidmore, a young assignment editor working in the newsroom. She asked if Donny was still in the green room. She was a huge fan and was going to see if she could leave the assignment desk to come upstairs to see him in person. In a follow-up call, a disappointed Rosalva told me she could not get away. I walked across the hall and stepped into the green room. Donny Osmond stood up when I entered. I introduced myself and asked if he could do me a favor. He said, "Absolutely." After his interview concluded, Donny came back upstairs to my office and said, "Let's do it." Normally, celebrities left the station by way of the main hallway and didn't enter the newsroom, but Donny and I went outside the studio to a walkway that led directly to the newsroom. As I led him through to the assignment desk, a lot of heads turned but not Rosalva's. She was talking on the phone at the assignment desk and looking down. When we reached the desk, Rosalva looked up and dropped the phone. Donny introduced himself to her and spent several minutes talking with her; all the while, Rosalva looked like she was living that Technicolor dream. I walked Donny out to the Columbia Square parking lot, thanked him, and said he made Rosalva's day. He replied, "And she made mine."

Chapter 39

Famous Guests and Encounters

Channel 2 did a "Pet of the Week" segment during Steve Edwards's noon broadcast. The pet, a dog or cat, was available for adoption, and each week, a different celebrity would appear with the pet and give out the animal shelter information where the rescue could take place. It happened I was having work done in my home, and I couldn't leave my dog, Kelly, so I brought her to work. I adopted Kelly through the Doris Day Pet Foundation. She was a tricolored mixed breed, part Australian Shepherd, part who knows, bigger than a Sheltie and smaller than a Collie. She spent most of the day stretched out on the floor of my office, only to lift her head, wag her tail, and greet visitors who came in for research. My research office was located down the hall from the makeup department. On-air guests passed by my door on their way to makeup. One such celebrity guest was actress Betty White. She spotted Kelly as she started to pass my door. Betty is famous for her work with animals and her contributions to the Los Angeles Zoo. She walked into my office, got down on her hands and knees so that she was face to face with Kelly, and told her, "Oh, we will find a good home for you." Kelly loved every minute of it. Betty thought Kelly was the Pet of the

Week. I quickly explained to her that Kelly was my dog and was just visiting my office for the day.

I've met several politicians, celebrities, mayors, and governors over the years, and people have asked who was most impressive. Without a doubt, that would be Israeli Prime Minister Shimon Peres. He had an aura about him that, on meeting him and shaking his hand, I knew I was in the presence of a great man, a world leader. It was overwhelming being in the company of such a man, but he was warm and down to earth.

One time, South African surgeon Dr. Christiaan Barnard, the first to perform a successful human heart transplant, was at the station for an interview. It was an honor to shake the hand that had saved so many lives.

Among the prominent women I met were Sally Ride (the first American woman in space), Maureen O'Hara, and Dolly Parton. I would say the most striking was actress Sophia Loren. She came to the station for an interview. I've never seen a more beautiful woman, her skin, her bone structure, and her class. She was a warm, friendly person to everyone on the news staff.

Presidential candidate Hubert Humphrey proved to be a humorous, charming presence, sitting on top of our desks, chatting and perhaps flirting with news administrator Bette Penny. Upon being introduced to Bette, he picked up on her last name and said, "And a mighty pretty penny it is too." Bette, who had copper-colored hair and a vivacious personality to go with it, loved every minute of the exchange with Humphrey.

NBC's late-night host Johnny Carson paid Channel 2 a surprise visit when we were taping a show honoring guest Ed McMahon's birthday. Johnny hung around the set after we finished taping, and our business manager, Millie DuVal, said to him, "You are keeping me up more nights than my husband."

Johnny Carson replied, "Well then, he'd better get a better act."

Our entertainment reporter, Gary Franklin, introduced me to a young, handsome man with dark hair and the bluest eyes I'd ever seen, a rising star named John Travolta. He was shy and obviously new to doing television interviews. Someone else Gary brought to my attention: Julia Roberts, who had accompanied her brother to the station for his interview. Gary interviewed Eric Roberts, but told me later the sister would be someone to watch.

Chapter 40

The Wheel

The "News Wheel" was a disastrous programming concept signed off by the powers that be in New York. For two hours, a revolving set (hence the name) with twenty-minute reports on such topics as health, my town/your town, and entertainment was interspersed with news of the day. One might expect glitches on debut day, but each day got progressively worse. Critics wrote scathing reviews. Channel 2's viewers wrote letters and phoned, complaining about the new concept. Although it wasn't just the idea of the general manager and news director, they were both sent packing. The "News Wheel" debuted in September 1986 and was cancelled in October, lasting only a month.

Chapter 41

Jose Rios: Open-Door Policy

Station management decided a news director didn't always have to come from another city but could be promoted within the newsroom. Jose Rios was named our new news director in 1990. Jose worked his way up to management. He started in the newsroom as a news associate on the assignment desk, eventually becoming assignment desk manager. Jose was a hands-on manager, well liked and respected by all. Jose was approachable and employed an open-door policy. But before he had time to make inroads in news ratings, he was replaced. Once again, a new station management came in with a new news director from another city, a new set, and anchor changes. What management never seemed to realize is that viewers like consistency—anchor faces they become familiar with, television news delivery from those they have come to know and welcome daily into their living rooms.

Chapter 42

Newsmakers

One Channel 2 news director, John Lippman, asked me to take over the producer's role on *Newsmakers* (a local *Face the Nation*-type broadcast), which aired weekly in the early 1990s. I was challenged by taking on the job and very fortunate to work with director James Nash and editor Allan Pena. I built the program around a topic in the news that week, and anchors Tritia Toyota, Bob Jimenez, and Mike Tuck rotated hosting the broadcast. I received two Emmy nominations for producing *Newsmakers*. My favorite show was about "Ethics in the News," which focused on how the media covered the Michael Jackson case. I invited as panelists actor Tom Selleck, who was actively involved in USC's ethics studies program, David Shaw of the *Los Angeles Times*, Channel 2's on-air legal expert, Harvey Levin, and anchor Tritia Toyota. We were midway through taping when James and I noticed something that looked like a statue appearing over Harvey Levin's shoulder. *Newsmakers* didn't have its own set; we borrowed the set from weekly KCBS, Channel 2 program, *Today's Religion*. The stage crew cleared out that show's backdrop and replaced it with the *Newsmakers* set, but that day, one item, a gleaming white statue of the Madonna, remained. Too late into taping, we continued. It was a lively broadcast, drew viewer praise, and James and I garnered another Emmy nomination as well as Press Club recognition.

With Tom Selleck on the Newsmakers set

My most embarrassing *Newsmakers* broadcast was the program devoted to the Los Angeles mayor's race. I want to make it clear: I was assigned by the news director to produce a broadcast because the "station needed to be able to check off a blank on a license renewal form." The news director said I could have no graphics or set, just studio backdrop curtains and pretaped introductions by anchors Tritia Toyota and Mike Tuck. Each candidate would have three minutes. Jim Nash and I thought the timing would work; however, when have you ever heard of a politician talking within his or her allotted time? It doesn't happen; usually, they go on and on—but not this time. Too many spoke *fewer* than three minutes, and a couple of candidates failed to show up, although their press aides did call. Our anchors returned to tape explanations about the no-show candidates. When the LA press corps turned out to witness this so-called debate, they found no set, just chairs set up. There were no anchors because they had both taped their introductions to the candidates the day before. Our "mayoral debate" aired on a Saturday night; it ran short, and to fill time, the station ran promotional spots for twenty minutes. James Nash and I were called to the general manager's office on Monday. We explained the limitations put on us and that the news director, who was already on borrowed time and was replaced sometime later, tied our hands. There were twenty-four mayoral candidates that year. Among the twenty-four candidates were colorful LA figures "Melrose" Larry Green and Eileen Anderson. Anderson was known in Los Angeles as the singing and dancing candidate. She had red hair, wore colorful outfits, and sang and danced an Irish jig on the streets of downtown Los Angeles. She showed up for the *Newsmakers* taping in more reserved attire and delivered her three-minute candidate pitch, ending with her campaign theme: "Show love to the people." Richard Riordan won the mayoral election.

Chapter 43

Tough Times

Channel 2 News in LA went through some bad times. So bad, in fact, that the station was making news—and not good news. We were in third place in the ratings among network-owned Los Angeles stations. A newsroom argument between anchor Mike Tuck and news director John Lippman became public. The news staffers who witnessed it broke it up. Both men agreed it was a heat-of-the-moment incident, and they were actually good friends. In a lighter moment, an outline of a victim formed in yellow police homicide tape was in front of Tuck's desk when he arrived in the newsroom the following morning. Although he had his critics in the newsroom, John Lippman brought an openness in that he decided to hold morning news staff meetings in the newsroom. Previous news directors held the morning meetings in their offices with producers. Lippman insisted everyone attend his meetings and contribute news story ideas., rather than simply following what appeared in the morning edition of the Los Angeles Times. Many good story ideas came out of those morning meetings. His tenure lasted sixteen months. He later joined Univision.

Chapter 44

Manson

August 9, 1969, was the date of one of the bloodiest, most notorious murders in the history of Los Angeles. Charles Manson directed his followers, which included three young women—Susan Atkins, Linda Kasabian, and Patricia Krenwinkel—and Tex Watson, to go on a brutal killing spree that Manson labeled "Helter Skelter." The first target was the home rented by director Roman Polanski at 10050 Cielo Drive, Beverly Hills. Polanski was out of the country, but the home was occupied by his eight-month pregnant wife, actress Sharon Tate, and her guests, hairstylist Jay Sebring, screenwriter Wojciech Frykowski, and his friend, coffee heiress Abigail Folger. Eighteen-year-old student Steven Parent was killed on the driveway leading to the property. Parent had visited a friend staying in the property's guesthouse and was leaving when he encountered the Manson Family killers.

The next night, August 10, the killing spree continued in the Silver Lake area of Los Angeles, where the Manson group found Leno and Rosemary LaBianca in their home at 3301 Waverly Drive in the Los Feliz district. Manson and his family of followers had been staking out the Waverly Drive homes in order to commit robberies. Businessman LaBianca and his wife had just returned from a trip to Lake Isabella.

Rosemary, age thirty-eight, retired to the bedroom, while Leno, forty-four, had fallen asleep on a couch while reading a newspaper. Manson and Watson broke into the home; Manson went into the bedroom and woke up Rosemary, while Watson stayed with Leno in the living room. Manson left the house, and Patricia Krenwinkel and Leslie Van Houten entered and joined Watson. Both LaBiancas were stabbed multiple times. When authorities entered the LaBianca home, they found the words "Healter Skelter" [sic] on the refrigerator door and "Death to Pigs" on the wall, written in Leno LaBianca's blood.

The killers were captured when a reporter from KABC, Al Wiman, and his crew traced the route Wiman suspected the killers had taken from the Cielo Drive location and drove along Benedict Canyon. Wiman figured the killers had discarded their bloody clothes somewhere over the canyon. He timed how long it took to change clothes and where the turnout would be where the killers could pull over and throw the clothes. He was right. He found bloody jeans and called Los Angeles police. Manson, Watson, Krenwinkel, Atkins, and Van Houten were convicted and given the death sentence in 1971. Chief Justice Rose Bird and the California Supreme Court overturned the death sentence, and they were sentenced to life in prison. Deputy District Attorney Stephen Kay, who was devoted to seeing they were never paroled, attended parole hearings for Manson and the Manson Family members. He accompanied Sharon Tate's mother, Doris, to the hearings. I spoke to Sharon's mother by telephone. Doris had become an advocate for crime victims and campaigned for the rights of crime victims and parents of murdered children. President George H. W. Bush honored her for her work in promoting victims' rights. After their mother became too ill to attend the parole hearings, Sharon's sisters Debra and Patti attended parole hearings for Manson and his followers in an effort to keep them behind bars. In 1986, California voters voted to remove Rose Bird and two other judges from the California Supreme Court.

Chapter 45

The Hillside Strangler

The series of murders began October 16, 1977, with the discovery of a young woman's body on an LA-area hillside. No attempt had been made to conceal the body. Nine more murders, all young girls and women, ages ranging from twelve to twenty-eight, occurred between October 1977 and February 1978. The discovery of the murder victims was the same. They were left in plain sight on LA hillsides. Thus, the media gave the serial murders a title: the case of the Hillside Strangler. The story led our Channel 2 News broadcasts every night. In the beginning, it was thought to be the work of one man. The Los Angeles police, Los Angeles Sheriff's Department and the Glendale police. formed a task force. Since some of the early victims were prostitutes, the theory was that a serial killer was targeting these types of women. That was until two new victims, parochial school girls, aged twelve and fourteen, became victims. The girls had been waiting at a bus stop where a witness saw them getting into a vehicle with two men. Law enforcement investigators got a break when they questioned upholstery shop owner Angelo Buono Jr. Buono and his cousin Kenneth Bianchi had teamed up to commit rape, torture, and murder over a two-month period. Bianchi fled to Bellingham, Washington, where he killed two more women after luring them to a home under the pretense he was looking to hire them for a house-sitting job. Bianchi agreed to plead guilty and testify against Buono in exchange for leniency and to avoid the death penalty. Buono was arrested October 22, 1979. He was convicted and sentenced to life in prison. He died of a heart attack in 2002 at California's Calipatria State Prison. Bianchi is serving a life sentence at Washington State Penitentiary in Walla Walla, Washington.

Chapter 46

Richard Ramirez: The Night Stalker

In the spring and summer of 1985, serial killer Richard Ramirez, who chose his victims randomly, terrorized residents of Los Angeles and Orange County. He crept in at night through unlocked windows and used knives, guns, and fists to exert violent death and physical and emotional pain. A Satan worshiper who committed thirteen murders, eleven sexual assaults, and fourteen burglaries, his violent spree was marked by pentagrams scrawled at crime scenes. His victims ranged in age from twenties to sixties. Some victims survived and were able to give police descriptions of the man who was dubbed "The Night Stalker" because his crimes occurred during the middle of the night. A San Francisco hotel manager identified Ramirez as a man who had stayed at his hotel for a brief period. But Ramirez had already left for Arizona to visit a brother. Upon his return to Los Angeles, he was recognized near a downtown bus station. Residents in an East Los Angeles neighborhood saw Ramirez trying to steal cars, ran after him, and captured and held him down until police arrived.

Ramirez could best be termed "The Face of Evil." During his Los Angeles criminal court trial, he disrupted court proceedings more than once by yelling out, "Hail Satan!" and holding up his hand to show cameras the pentagram drawn on it. His 1989 trial cost Los Angeles County $1.8 million. Jurors convicted Ramirez, and he received the death sentence. He was on San Quentin's Death Row until 2013, when he died of natural causes at age fifty-three.

Chapter 47

Menendez: Murder in Beverly Hills

On August 20, 1989, entertainment executive Jose Menendez and his wife, Kitty, were home in their Beverly Hills mansion on North Elm Drive watching a movie in their den. Suddenly, and without warning, Jose was shot in the back of the head. The shooter fired a twelve-gauge shotgun. Detectives theorized Kitty had fallen asleep on the couch, woke up to the sound of gunfire, and tried to run to the hallway. She was shot in the leg and fell. She was then shot several times in her chest, arm, and face. The couple had two young sons, Lyle, twenty-one, and Erik, eighteen, who told police they were out for the evening and came home to find their parents murdered. The story got considerable coverage, including the couple's funeral with TV footage of the two Menendez orphans, Lyle and Erik, arriving at the services for their murdered parents. There was some speculation that Jose and Kitty may have been killed by organized crime figures; Jose was CEO of LIVE Entertainment, Inc. However, no connection was made by law enforcement.

My job was to maintain an active research file. The story wasn't over, and there could be a sudden request from the desk in the event of breaking news. I built a file that contained all that was known about the Menendez murders, and most importantly, I added the home address—the scene of the murders—to the front of the file folder, along with important contact phone numbers. My file also contained the LA coroner's autopsy reports. The story broke again on March 8, 1990, when Lyle Menendez was arrested, charged with the murder of his parents, Jose and Kitty Menendez. I got a call from the assignment editor to bring the Menendez file because it had everything, including the address of the crime scene. Our reporter and crew were out the door and at the Menendez mansion before any station in town. I'm proud to say we were ahead of everyone.

The arrest of Lyle Menendez for the murder of his parents came about as a lucky break for police. Brother Erik confessed the murder to his therapist in Beverly Hills. The therapist's girlfriend was listening in from the next room. She called Beverly Hills police and repeated what she had overheard in her boyfriend's office. When Lyle was arrested, his brother Erik was in Israel but returned to Los Angeles three days later and surrendered.

The brothers had ambushed their parents in hopes of gaining their fortune. They disposed of the twelve-gauge shotguns on Mulholland Drive, then drove to a local movie theater and bought tickets to provide an alibi. Following the movie, they met friends at a local Cheesecake Factory restaurant to add to their alibi. Upon arriving at the mansion, Lyle dialed 911 and cried, "Someone has killed my parents." During the months following the murders, the Menendez brothers spent lavishly on overseas trips, Rolex watches, a Porsche Carrera, and penthouse apartments in Marina del Rey. They went through one million dollars in six months.

The brothers' trial was delayed until a determination could be made about whether the tape recordings of Erik's sessions with his psychiatrist were admissible. Judge James Albrecht ruled they could be admitted because Lyle violated the physician-patient privilege when he threatened harm to Erik's therapist. The first trial ended in deadlock; the brothers were tried together but had separate juries. The retrial didn't focus on the defense used in the first, which was sexual and psychological abuse. Jurors saw the horrific crime scene photos of Jose, and particularly of Kitty, who was attacked so violently she was unrecognizable. Jurors convicted the brothers of murder in the first degree, with special circumstances of lying-in-wait and multiple murders. The jury chose life in prison without the possibility of parole for both men. Lyle married twice (in 1996, divorced in 2001, and again in 2003), and Erik married once (in 1999), both to women who corresponded with them in prison.

Chapter 48

Michael Jackson: King of Pop

I was already home when my phone rang. It was our producer, Michael Horowicz. He said I should come back to the station as soon as possible. When you work in news, you don't really conform to a schedule. If there's a breaking news story, then you don't call in, you come in. This was the situation numerous times while I worked in news—for example, the Cerritos midair crash that occurred on a Labor Day holiday, and of course, any earthquakes, fires, train accidents, and plane crashes. I drove the Ventura (101) Freeway from Encino to the Hollywood Freeway and back to the station. When I arrived, Michael told me our assignment desk had a tip that the Santa Barbara Sheriff's Department was going to conduct a raid at entertainer Michael Jackson's Neverland Ranch, located near Los Olivos, in Santa Barbara County. I worked in the newsroom late into the night, gathering research about Jackson's childhood, career, family, and many changes in appearance over the years; his overseas trips to perform at live concerts; and his Las Vegas life. In 1993, LAPD began an investigation based on a charge brought by a Beverly Hills dentist, Evan Chandler, that Jackson had allegedly molested his twelve-year-old son. No charges were filed, and the case was settled out of court. Chandler reportedly received a multimillion-dollar payment from Jackson to settle the case.

In 2003, child molestation charges were filed against Michael Jackson—charges that he molested a thirteen-year-old boy. I was no longer working in news but followed the Jackson trial coverage. Jackson was indicted and stood trial. He was acquitted of all charges. Michael Jackson died on June 25, 2009. He was fifty years old.

Chapter 49

KC, the Action News Cat

S he arrived at the station unannounced. With her sleek black coat, she wouldn't reveal her age. She was seen alone, wandering the street near the station at the intersection of Sunset and Gower. Ferd, one of our stage technicians, rescued her. A "temporary" home was created for her in a production area near the news broadcast studio. Everyone contributed to a fund to pay for her food and vet bills. We named her KCBS...KC for short. She easily became a permanent fixture as the station mascot: KC, the Action News Cat.

She would climb the stairs on the TV side of our building, make her way to the second-floor hallway, and head straight to the makeup room. KC would jump up into one of the chairs in makeup artist Joanna's room, curl up, and go to sleep. No one wanted to disturb her. When on-air talent (guest artists, politicians, whoever) arrived for makeup, another chair would be brought to the area for their use. KC would often come down the hallway to my news research office, crawl into a chair in front of the NEXIS computer, and sleep. When anyone came in to use the computer, another chair would be found for their use in order not to move KC. She could often be seen resting atop the studio control room panel. When she tired of the television side of the Columbia Square building, she would cross the hall and wait by the elevator to join someone on the ride up to KNX Radio News. In other words, KC went wherever she felt like going and was mostly always welcomed. I say mostly because there were two people who didn't like having her around: one was a television production manager and the other an on-air personality. KC seemed to recognize that fact and would invariably enter the news broadcast set about the time this latter individual was ready to go on the air. She was never seen on camera but would wander around the set during the live broadcast. Both people left Channel 2 for other pursuits, but KC was still very much around. It became normal to see employees stop in the hallway to talk to KC when she was making her rounds. "How are you today, KC?" was often heard.

KC the Action News Cat

Chapter 50

The Big Earthquake of
January 17, 1994, 4:31 a.m.

I awoke to a thundering sound, my house shaking as though a train had hit it and was dragging it down the tracks. It lasted ten to twenty seconds. The power was off. I managed to make my way from my bed to a crank-out window that faced the street in front of my house. I heard a woman's voice outside asking if everyone was all right; she carried a flashlight, and when I called out, she approached my window and shined the light in so that I could see. My bedroom furniture was all toppled over. My dog, Kelly, who slept in a corner to the right of my bed, was pinned behind a dresser. A couple of men who were visiting neighbors across the street came over and lifted my furniture. Kelly, thankfully, was unharmed and came out wagging her tail. I needed to leave immediately for work.

The block wall fence around the back and sides of my house had collapsed. A section of ceiling in my den had crashed to the floor. My refrigerator took a walk, the door had swung open, and its contents lay on the floor. Phones weren't working. I put Kelly in my car, and on my way down the driveway, my neighbor handed me a cup of Turkish coffee. I'd never tried it before, but it really tasted good, and more importantly, was comforting. I drove a couple of blocks over to a friend's home. She offered to keep Kelly for me since her fence was still standing.

It was fortunate that the quake occurred so early in the morning. Children were not in school, and traffic was light. I drove the Ventura Freeway to the Hollywood Freeway and into work at Columbia Square. What met my eyes when I arrived was shocking. Built in the 1930s, the newsroom was located in the former Columbia Records recording studio. Parts of the asbestos tile ceiling were down, and desks were covered with dust. The studio lights had collapsed, and the monitors had toppled. But Channel 2 News was on the air, broadcasting breaking details as they came in. Anchor Tritia Toyota was first on the air because of our emergency generator. There were fires all over the city, particularly in the San Fernando Valley, where the epicenter in Reseda was located. I lived in Encino, the next community over from Reseda. The earthquake was named the Northridge Quake because there was so much damage to that community. There were fifty-seven killed, eighty-seven hundred injured, and an estimated twenty billion dollars in damage. A section of the Santa Monica Freeway collapsed, as did the Antelope Valley Freeway where LAPD officer Clarence Wayne Dean was killed when he mistakenly drove his motorcycle off the collapsed section in his haste to get to work.

When the quake hit at 4:31 a.m., the station was staffed but only at a minimum. By 6:30 a.m., the newsroom was fully staffed. There were several strong aftershocks, and staffers ducked under their desks. In my office, the top of the Xerox machine had broken off, flown up, and landed on top of the file cabinets. The magazines and papers in the research library had collapsed into a pile. The tape library looked as though someone had backed a two-ton truck into it and unloaded a mound of videotape. After many hours of gathering information for air from local hospitals and public officials, someone in the newsroom asked about KC, the Action News Cat. We searched for her with no results, but later that day, she wandered into the newsroom unscathed, and we breathed a collective sigh of relief.

All the LA news stations provided good, up-to-date coverage. But our Channel 2 coverage was the leader because of that generator and excellent anchor work by Tritia Toyota and our staff. We were awarded Golden Mikes from the Los Angeles Radio and Television Association for Live Coverage of Breaking News.

With anchors Chris Conangla and Tritia Toyota

Chapter 51

The O. J. Simpson Criminal Trial

I covered both Simpson trials: the criminal trial in downtown Los Angeles, and later, the civil trial in Santa Monica, which was nicknamed O. J. by the Sea by journalists.

On Sunday night, June 12, 1994, Nicole Brown Simpson and her family dined at Mezzaluna restaurant in Brentwood after attending a dance performance at her daughter's school. Nicole's mother, Judita, left her eyeglasses behind, so Ron Goldman, a waiter at the restaurant, offered to bring them to Nicole's residence. Nicole Brown Simpson and Ron Goldman were discovered brutally murdered outside Nicole's condo on June 13, 1994. LAPD detectives theorized Goldman was a victim because he was in the wrong place at the wrong time.

Nicole, thirty-five, was the ex-wife of the "Juice," a nickname for Heisman-winning, former USC football player Orenthal James Simpson, known to the world as O. J. He was an actor, a popular and well-known ad man for Hertz, and the father of Nicole's two children, Sydney, nine, and Justin, six. I had a research file on Nicole and O. J., and among other items, it contained the *Herald-Examiner* newspaper issue of New Year's Day 1989, headlining the assault on

Nicole by O. J., accompanied by a photo of her bruised and battered face. During trial testimony, it was disclosed that Nicole had a safety deposit box containing the same edition of the *Herald*. She had saved it as evidence against O. J.

In our 9:00 a.m. news staff meeting, we talked about the Brentwood murders and that one of the victims was Simpson's ex-wife. I brought my Simpson research file to the staff meeting and spoke about O. J.'s threats to and abuse of Nicole. Our news director said, "Who cares? Let's move on." Of course, he was proven wrong—the public cared. The case, along with massive media coverage of the trial, became a topic of discussion nationally, with some believing Simpson was innocent. In the beginning, when I learned O. J. was on a flight to Chicago, I, too, felt he couldn't be the perpetrator. Simpson retained Attorney Howard Weitzman. At first, it looked like a slam dunk for Simpson to be released. But as the time line developed, LAPD detectives Tom Lange and Philip Vannatter showed that O. J. had enough time to commit the murders, return to his home in Brentwood, shower, climb into the limo waiting outside his home, and still make his flight to Chicago out of LAX. There was also the matter of a witness. Jill Shively claimed she saw O. J. in his white Ford Bronco with its headlights off at the intersection of San Vicente and Bundy the night of the murders. Prosecutor Marcia Clark decided not to call Shively to the witness stand because Shively sold her story to a tabloid, which sparked discussion in the newsroom.

Weitzman decided not to defend O. J., so he hired a team of attorneys headed by Johnnie Cochran. As one of my best contacts in the LA district attorney's office, I knew Johnnie well. He was a former prosecuting attorney in the DA's office, and we discussed many cases during his prosecutorial days. Cochran added attorney Robert

Shapiro and built a strong defense lineup of Robert Kardashian, F. Lee Bailey, Alan Dershowitz, Gerald Uelmen, Carl Douglas, Robert Blasier, and DNA experts Barry Scheck and Peter Neufeld—the so-called dream team. I researched the panel of jurors and alternates to learn where they lived and what they did professionally, so when the verdict was announced, Channel 2's reporters could be first to interview them. Jurors were off-limits during the trial; they couldn't be followed home, or the offending news station would lose its credentials. But it was vital that I have background on each juror and be ready to go when the verdict came in, and Judge Ito declared jurors were free to speak to the media. My job was to research background of every player in the Simpson trial and to provide research information to our assignment desk, reporters, and anchors in preparation for coverage of what turned out to be the most televised criminal trial in US history.

The media nicknamed the courthouse in downtown LA "Camp O. J." It was there I briefly met with Simpson's lead attorney, Johnnie Cochran, in the court hallway to set up an interview with our new reporter, Beverly Burke, who wanted to discuss his career leading up to the O. J. case. Since we were old friends, Cochran agreed to meet with Beverly and sit down for a one-on-one interview; however, discussion of the case was off-limits. Burke and I both adhered to court edicts and avoided any discussion of the trial whatsoever.

The O. J. criminal trial ran from November 2, 1994, when a panel of twelve jurors was selected, until the verdict was announced October 3, 1995. The jurors deliberated fewer than four hours, and there was tension in the courtroom as the jury's decision was announced: not guilty. Ron Goldman's father, Fred, and sister, Kim, were devastated. There was a shocked look on the face of Robert

With planning director Akila Gibbs and reporter Bevely Burke

Kardashian. Simpson's trial was the last story I covered at KCBS Channel 2 News. I worked past the retirement date at the request of the news director and general manager. Both wanted me to stay past June, and I agreed to stay through Simpson's trial.

Chapter 52

Momentary Retirement

L eaving KCBS Channel 2 News was bittersweet for me. Along with many other CBS employees, I was offered an enhanced retirement package. I could accept or decline. I really wasn't ready to retire. However, I considered the offer very carefully. As general manager in the 1990s, Bill Applegate did not want me to take the retirement package I was offered. But it was a one-time offer from Mr. Tisch, who wanted to make the books look good so that Westinghouse would take over CBS. My offer was enhanced by five years to my length of service and five years to my age in order to arrive at quite a substantial figure. Bill called me to his office and begged me to stay through the O. J. trial rather than leaving in June. He didn't want to lose my valuable research skills, he said. He proposed that if I was going to leave, then I should set up an outside news research service and contract with CBS and every other station in town. He suggested I open an office on Ventura Boulevard and hire messengers and other research personnel. It was very flattering. I did consider the proposal, but in the long run, I thought it would be too large an undertaking. I hated leaving when I did, but the enhanced pension offer was not going to be there in the future. I accepted the offer.

With Bob Long and Mike Daniels at my retirement party

With Jerry Dunphy at my retirement party

Later, I came back to Channel 2 for a friend's retirement party. News director Larry Perret saw me, greeted me warmly, and said he wanted me to meet with investigative reporter Joel Grover, a new addition to Channel 2's news staff. I met with Joel, and Larry wanted to hire me back to work in the investigative unit. Under IRS rules, I couldn't come back to work for the same company, or my enhanced pension would be reduced. The rule was complicated. When he ran the request by CBS New York, the answer came back no, the reason being the IRS rules stating I couldn't work for the same company; if I did, then I would lose the enhanced portion of my pension. Channel 2's business office tried to work around it, but the answer was still a firm no. CBS Network News based at Television City also wanted to hire me. When CBS bureau chief Jennifer Siebens learned she couldn't hire me, she phoned the ABC News bureau chief on the West Coast and suggested he hire me. Clem Lane called me to come in for an interview at ABC News. Wanting to make a good impression, I dressed up in a suit and heels. I met with Clem Lane and assistant bureau chief David Eaton. The two wanted me to start work at ABC News the following Monday. I asked what the dress code was, and the two laughed and said, "Casual. We both thought you were going out following your interview here."

Bureau chief Clem Lane of ABC News was one of the finest, sharpest men I ever worked with. Clem had a rich sense of humor. He loved music and news and talking about both. Lane came from a news background: his father, John Lane, was a top CBS News executive for many years, and his grandfather and namesake was longtime city editor of the *Chicago Daily News*. Clem Lane was supportive, and he and the ABC News Los Angeles bureau were welcoming to me, offering to help me in any way they could. Working with them was, to coin an old phrase, the icing on the cake following my retirement from Channel 2, KCBS, Los Angeles. I learned that Clem Lane died May 13, 2011. He was fifty years old and had been with ABC News for twenty-five years.

Chapter 53

Cancer: The News No One Wants to Hear

A few days following my retirement from CBS, I found time to see a gynecologist for a routine checkup. During my exam, Dr. Torbarina of Tarzana Medical Center said she saw a buildup of the lining of my uterus. Since we had done several news stories about gynecological cancer and I knew that this was one of the symptoms, I thought, *Oh, no.* Dr. Torbarina said, "If you're thinking of cancer, I don't see any sign of that." However, she said she was taking a tissue sample in order to do a biopsy. The next day, I was packing my luggage for a trip to Atlanta to see the kids for Christmas when my phone rang. It was Dr. Torbarina who said, "I have really bad news. You have uterine cancer. You will be seeing Dr. Richard Friedman, a gynecological oncologist." I told her I was packing to leave for Atlanta. She replied, "No, you are going in for surgery now."

I want to emphasize that I had *no* symptoms when I got the news no one wants to hear: a cancer diagnosis. My pap smears had been normal. My experience is similar to actress/comedienne Fran Drescher's. I've seen interviews she's done about her uterine cancer and how it took many doctor visits before a biopsy was done and a correct diagnosis was made. She writes about overcoming cancer in her best-selling book *Cancer Schmancer*. I was lucky that Dr. Torbarina decided to do a biopsy. She saved my life. And I cannot say enough about my surgeon, Dr. Richard Friedman, a gynecologist/oncologist. He continued to see me postsurgery, first at Tarzana Medical, then in his new office at Hollywood Presbyterian, and later at the Disney Cancer Center in Burbank. I saw him initially every three months, then six, and finally yearly, up until I moved from Encino. I have a photo we took in his office, and it remains on my bookcase. He will always be in my heart. Make those gynecology appointments and get checked, even though you may not be experiencing symptoms.

When I learned of Elizabeth Edwards's cancer diagnosis, I wrote to her from my position as a cancer survivor; I didn't write her about politics (as she was the wife of presidential candidate Senator John Edwards of North Carolina). I wrote a note of support and encouragement. Not expecting a reply, I received one, and it was handwritten. The date was February 7, 2005. The letter reads:

Dear Lorraine, you are inspiring. Thank you for your support. You understand, I know, how much it has meant to me. Hearing your story gives me courage and hope. I am almost through my chemotherapy treatment, and am tolerating it well, particularly with John at my side at every treatment. I expect to be through radiation treatment by June and to have hair by August. Your support means so much to me and to my family. John and I do have the sense that, as with our past and future battles, you are with us in this one.

Warmest Wishes,
Elizabeth Edwards

John Edwards admitted to an extramarital affair in 2008, after the tabloids ran several stories about him and a woman named Rielle Hunter. Edwards had hired Hunter in 2006 to shoot documentaries on his campaign trips. Elizabeth announced a separation, with intention to file for divorce. Edwards admitted he had fathered Rielle Hunter's baby. Elizabeth Edwards died December 7, 2010.

Chapter 54

ABC News: Back to the Newsroom

After I retired from CBS, Channel 2 News, I received a call from a producer at EXTRA, an entertainment news locally produced daily broadcast. Some former Channel 2 staffers were now working at EXTRA and had recommended me. I went to EXTRA's production office for an interview.

Another opportunity came from Southwest Airlines. It was to work in public relations, based at Burbank (now Bob Hope) Airport.

A third offer came from Valley College to teach a journalism class.

However, before I could seriously consider any offers, the call came from ABC News to come to work in their Los Angeles bureau as the director of news research on the O. J. Simpson civil trial case. I oversaw the comparison of witnesses and major trial figures depositions, including Simpson's. When testimony was taking place, I informed ABC's correspondents about changes in what was said in the earlier depositions versus current testimony. A week after I joined ABC, Lydia Boyle from *Dateline* joined our team. While I had contacts in the DA's office and the LAPD, Lydia was my counterpart; she had contacts on the defense side. She was friends with O. J.'s sports rep of many years, Michael Gilbert, and with his sisters Carmelita and Shirley. Lydia and I quickly bonded and became close friends.

Getting the trial jurors' backgrounds was the toughest part of my research job. I might have a tidbit of information to go on. In doing news research over the years, I found it was fairly simple to learn anything about anyone. But these jurors were a different matter. I knew from the court releases of information some basic information: the makeup of how many men and how many women, race, and sometimes age. Media, under court order from Judge Hiroshi Fujisaki, and correctly so, was not to approach, follow, contact, or otherwise attempt interference with the selected jurors. One LA station had a researcher who followed one of the jurors, and that station lost its courtroom credentials as a result. I'm proud of the job I did, since I was responsible for ABC News having names and locations of all twelve jurors. We were ready to go when the verdict was read, and Judge Hiroshi Fujisaki dismissed them. ABC News, being competitive and wanting to get the interviews first, sent out letters to jurors as soon as the verdict came down. *Good Morning America* anchors Joan Lunden and Charles Gibson signed letters to the jurors, as did Barbara Walters. No one could predict what time of day the verdict would be coming. We were prepared for *Nightline*, *GMA*, *Nightly News* with Peter Jennings, and so on. We had commitments from LAPD detectives Tom Lange and Phil Vannatter to do interviews for all of ABC's news programs. When the verdict came down, the two detectives arrived at ABC's newsroom to do interviews as promised.

It was 1996, and ABC News and *Good Morning America* wanted me to do an interview with Kris Jenner, who was one of Nicole Brown Simpson's closest girlfriends. I phoned Kris, and she invited me to come to the home she shared with her husband, Bruce, in Hidden Hills. Kris welcomed me, and we sat in her living room. She could not have been nicer. She asked that we talk quietly because her baby was asleep nearby. She looked fabulous for just having had a baby, her daughter Kendall with Bruce. She had three daughters and a son with ex-husband Robert Kardashian (a member of O. J.'s dream team). Two years later, she gave birth to Kylie, her second daughter with Bruce. She related to me an incident that happened during a party she and Bruce had in their home. O. J. and Nicole were guests at the party. O. J. had lost it, exploded, and was yelling at Nicole. Bruce and Kris asked him to leave. She said it had been a frightening incident.

Bruce came jogging into the room, carrying an energy drink. He was pleasant enough but wanted me to ask the executives at ABC and *Good Morning America* if they would publicize a book he was writing. I phoned our bureau chief at ABC News, who declined Bruce's request. I told Bruce there was no interest at this time and that I was there to discuss the Simpson case. My meeting at the Jenner home occurred long before Bruce Jenner's successful transition to becoming a woman and choosing the name Caitlyn.

On January 16, 1997, both sides rested. Jurors had heard 101 witnesses during forty-one days of testimony. O. J. Simpson testified for the first time before a jury on November 22, 1996, and took the stand again on January 10, 1997. The dream team of Cochran and company didn't represent him in the Santa Monica civil trial. His attorney was Robert Baker, whose closing argument was on January 22, 1997. The plaintiffs' attorney was Daniel Petrocelli, whose closing was January 21, 1997. On February 4, 1997, the Santa Monica jury found Simpson liable for the deaths of Nicole Brown Simpson and Ron Goldman and awarded the plaintiffs $33.5 million in compensatory and punitive damages.

While working at ABC News on the O. J. Simpson civil trial, I was asked to help the desk on a fatal shooting case that happened

January 16, 1997. We had the license plate number of the car belonging to the victim, so I called my contact at the DMV in Sacramento. I was informed the car was registered to Ennis Cosby, Bill and Camille Cosby's twenty-seven-year-old son. He was changing a tire on his Mercedes at 1:45 a.m. on Skirball Center Drive, near the 405 Freeway. Police theorized Ennis was shot in the head during a robbery attempt. Ukranian-born immigrant Mikhail Markhasev confessed to killing Cosby. He was convicted and, later, dropped any appeals, saying he wanted to make amends to Cosby's family and spare his own anguish. He is serving a mandatory life-without-parole sentence.

Chapter 55

Sinatra: Chairman of the Board

D uring my work for ABC News on the Simpson civil trial, Clem
Lane came to my office and asked if he could pull me away to
work on an obituary for Frank Sinatra. He was in the hospital. It was
January 6, 1997. The network wanted to be ready to air an obituary
should Sinatra die, but he recovered and left the hospital.

My friend Marie and I were teenage fans of Frank Sinatra. We
were a little young for the height of the bobby-soxer stage of screaming girls chasing after Sinatra at his various appearances, but during
his *Your Hit Parade* shows at NBC, located at the corner of Sunset and
Vine, we, being adventuresome girls, decided we would attempt to
attend a show and sit quietly in the audience. To make ourselves look
older, we donned nylon stockings, the style of the time with lines up
the back of the legs, and hooked on a garter belt. High heels were a
must, and did we wobble in them! We rolled our hair with rats (what
beauty operators used in women's hair to roll it up into large curls on
top of the head). The rats were made of some sort of stuffing material and wrapped in netting. We had these two giant curls on top that
met in the middle and were shaped like sausages. We waited in line
on the street in front of NBC and were delighted the ushers admitted us. However, I don't think our supposed grown-up appearance

fooled anyone. Sinatra was wonderful, along with Dorothy Collins, popular singer and regular *Your Hit Parade* performer.

I saw Sinatra on many occasions over the years. One night after work, I went with coworkers to the Villa Capri, an Italian restaurant a few blocks from the station. It was crowded, and we sat at the piano bar. Our seats turned out to be front row, since an impromptu performance from band leader Ray Conniff, a couple of members of his band, and the piano bar player, was joined by Sinatra who, like Conniff, happened to be dining at Villa Capri that night. No one moved from the piano bar. Sinatra had it all. His voice—every word of every lyric—could be understood. The emotion in his singing was all his. Throughout his career, he respected and paid tribute to musicians. I saw him again a few years later, also in a restaurant. I'd gone to Palm Springs for a weekend. A friend and I were having dinner at Sorrentino's, one of Sinatra's favorite Italian restaurants. He was also dining there. A pianist started to play "New York, New York" in tribute to Frank. Everyone in the restaurant stood up, linked arms, and sang and moved to the music. We may, in fact, have been one of the original "flash mobs." Frank Sinatra loved it. The next time I saw him was at the Golden Nugget in Las Vegas. He was performing in a small, intimate room. His show started around 9:00 p.m. and ended around 2:00 a.m. He was very nostalgic. He rested between numbers and spoke about some of his films, paying tribute to costars Rita Hayworth and Kim Novak in particular. He spoke about the recent death of his son-in-law. At the close of his performance, he spoke about the many musicians he had worked with, giving credit to each and every one for the success of his records over the years. It was an evening I'll never forget.

Sinatra was such a prominent figure throughout my life, and there I was assigned so many years later to write his obituary. The chairman of the board, as Sinatra was called, died May 14, 1998. He was eighty-two years old.

Chapter 56

A Lifetime of Travel

Throughout my life, I made many trips overseas to Greece, Italy, Germany, and England. In 1991, I signed up for a group tour to Russia. Two weeks before we were to depart, the August Coup took place, and the trip was very nearly canceled. Our number of forty lowered to twenty because some were leery of conditions in Moscow. Our tour guide told us the week before we arrived that there were tanks in the streets; however, everything worked out for us. We were able to tour the Armory in Moscow and the Hermitage in Saint Petersburg. We had a two-night stay in Kiev, the capital of Ukraine. And we witnessed a historic night in Saint Petersburg with the taking down of the Leningrad signs and the restoration of the city's name to Saint Petersburg.

A couple of US trips resulted in my writing travel columns. The first was my trip to Hawaii. I flew to Oahu and island-hopped from there. Since I went alone and met many interesting people along the way, I wrote a piece about it and submitted it for publication by the *Los Angeles Times* Sunday Travel Section. My second column, about a trip to Atlantic City, published by the *Los Angeles Herald-Express*, was a comparison of East Coast gambling casinos versus Las Vegas casinos, which were the travel destination of many Southern Californians.

In Moscow

I also visited the Twin Towers at the World Trade Center on three occasions. The first was when I was working for CBS at the 1976 Democratic Convention. Some coworkers and I took the elevator to the top where the restaurant Windows on the World on the 107th floor was located. We enjoyed drinks and dinner at sunset and looked out at the spectacular view: the Statue of Liberty and the Manhattan skyline. I'd been to New York City's 21, Russian Tea Room, Tavern on the Green, and Sign of the Dove restaurants, all special in their own way, but none could match the dining experience at Windows. In 1980, I was once again working in New York at the Democratic Convention at Madison Square Garden. I was invited to join coworkers for drinks and appetizers at Windows on the World at the Twin Towers. And lastly, in 1982, I was asked by my boss in Los Angeles to visit my research director counterpart at CBS in New York in order to plan and design my new research department at KCBS. I was asked to come along with a group from CBS Network News who were going to Windows on the World restaurant. The Twin Towers were the target of terrorists and were destroyed on September 11, 2001.

I have visited as many of our nation's presidential libraries as possible during my travels. Following my work stint for CBS at the Democratic and Republican Conventions, I would rent a car and spend a day exploring the historical sites near the city in which I was working. After the Republican Convention in Kansas City, I drove to Independence, Missouri, to visit the Harry Truman Library and Museum. President Truman is buried there, and although his home is nearby, I couldn't tour it because Mrs. Bess Truman, the president's widow, was living there at the time. Since her passing, the Truman residence has been opened for tours. While visiting DC, I toured Mount Vernon, and in Virginia, Jefferson's home. I found President Roosevelt's Hyde Park a beautiful area in upstate New

York. I've visited Roosevelt's Warm Springs, Georgia, "Little White House" on a number of occasions and am struck by how plain the furnishings are, in keeping with the depression era in which it was built. There is one simple guard house at the entrance, common in the days before heavy Presidential Secret Service protection. In Boston, I spent a day at the John F. Kennedy Library. Since I lived in Southern California, there were many visits to Ronald Reagan's Library and Museum located in Simi Valley and to Richard Nixon's in Yorba Linda. My goal now that I'm living in a suburb of Atlanta is to visit the Jimmy Carter Library and Museum.

Chapter 57

Reagan

When I started to write this memoir, I discovered how many events in my life are intertwined. From my childhood and teenage years to my work at CBS Television City to KNXT, Channel 2 News (later KCBS), and at ABC News, one name, Ronald Reagan, was always present. As a kid, I read a lot of movie magazines. Stars' pictures and articles about them were featured, planted by their press agents, managers, and the studios. I was already a fan of actor Ronald Reagan's, and the magazines filled in the gaps about him, such as his boyhood and his early career as a radio sportscaster. Reagan was a Warner Brothers Studio contract player. I decided to write him a fan letter detailing a dream I'd had about him wearing a leather jacket and holding a model ship. Much to my surprise, I received a hand-written letter from him in return along with an autographed personal photo. In the photo, taken on his patio, he made my dream a reality.

We exchanged letters and cards over a long period. At the time, he had just been elected president of the Screen Actors Guild. Reagan was married to actress Jane Wyman. The two were parents to daughter Maureen and adopted son Michael. Jane lost a third baby. Ronald Reagan wrote me that he thought the studio had forced

Ronald Reagan, autographed photo, 1947

Jane to go back to work too soon after the loss of their baby. He also wrote about some of the world's problems. When I asked about passes to come to the studio, he responded that it wouldn't look good for him as president of the Actors Guild to request passes, but he said, "Someday this world of ours will straighten out, and I can try again to get passes." I saved Reagan's correspondence and photos he mailed to me, photos taken on the patio of the home he shared with Wyman.

I saw Reagan many times over the years. The first was at the Carthay Circle Theatre where his film *Stallion Road* was premiering. I was in the first row of the bleachers watching the stars' arrival when Reagan and Wyman came over, greeted fans, and signed autograph books. It was an overwhelming experience for me. I saw him again at the Hollywood Bowl on a Sunday afternoon when he was a participant on stage during "I Am an American Day," a local patriotic event. Reagan came to KNXT, Channel 2, where I worked as the news director's secretary. He was a guest on *Newsmakers*, a local Los Angeles news program, when he was governor of California. I shared some of my pictures with the producer of *Newsmakers*. Reagan expressed surprise that we had those photos.

I saw him again in Detroit when I was covering the 1980 Republican Convention for CBS. Seeing him from the perspective of the convention floor was a hard experience to describe, but it took me briefly back to that day outside Carthay Circle and the memory that had nothing to do with politics. While I've saved the bulk of Reagan's handwritten correspondence to me, I did auction off one letter. It was auctioned by Profiles in History. I wanted to donate it to the Reagan Library in Simi Valley. The donation was to be in the names of my grandchildren. However, when I contacted a curator at the library, I was informed they wouldn't display a letter of that nature. There is very little on display about his first marriage to Jane Wyman; my letter from him spoke lovingly about her. It was written long before their divorce and his subsequent marriage to Nancy. Life for him was very different then. His long marriage to and devotion for Nancy are well known. They had a strong, loving marriage.

Nancy Reagan was at her husband's side at the Republican Convention in Detroit, along with his children, Maureen and Michael, from his first marriage to Jane, and Patti and Ron, his children with Nancy. His costar Jack Carson from his Warner Pictures days was also there.

Ronald Reagan was elected the fortieth president of the United States and served for eight years, from 1981 to 1989.

Sadly, I was to work on another story about Reagan: the assassination attempt by John Hinkley, age twenty-five. Hinkley, in his distorted mind, thought he could impress actress Jodie Foster, with whom he was obsessed. His intention was to kill the president so that he would be noticed. Hinkley shot President Reagan on March 30, 1981, outside the Washington Hilton Hotel. Reagan was sixty-nine days into his presidency. James Brady, Reagan's press spokesman, was also shot and was paralyzed. The president, although wounded, managed to joke with his surgeons. Reagan commented, "I hope you are all Republicans."

KCBS, Channel 2 News covered the opening of the Ronald Reagan Presidential Library in Simi Valley, California, on November 4, 1991. Ladybird Johnson; former President Jimmy Carter and his wife, Rosalynn; former President Gerald Ford and his wife, Betty; former President Richard Nixon and his wife, Pat; and former President George H. W. Bush and his wife, Barbara, attended the dedication. It was an amazing experience to witness them all present to honor Ronald and Nancy Reagan.

In November 1994, Channel 2 News once again had a breaking story about former President Reagan. He announced to the nation in the form of a handwritten letter that he had recently been diagnosed with Alzheimer's. He was eighty-three years old. Ronald Reagan died on June 5, 2004, at age ninety-three.

Chapter 58

The Bubble

I never dreamed I would make the decision to leave California. Born and raised in Los Angeles, I bought my home in Encino, a lovely section of the San Fernando Valley. In Southern California, one could drive to Santa Monica and the Pacific Ocean or visit Lake Arrowhead on the same day. Beach or snow. When driving on the 101 Ventura Freeway in sunny eighty-degree weather, I could see snowcapped mountains on the horizon ahead of me. I made the difficult decision to sell my home of thirty-five years. I had a lot of friends I would miss, but I was moving to be near my family, my grandchildren. I had become a frequent flier on Delta out of LAX, traveling to Atlanta for the kids' birthdays and for Christmas and vacations. After standing in line at LAX or on return flights out of Atlanta's Hartsfield Jackson Airport, I realized I no longer wanted to experience long lines or deal with luggage, and I needed to relocate.

I bought a home in Peachtree City, Georgia. Folks here in Peachtree City refer to it as "the Bubble." There is even a Facebook page called "Life in the Bubble." Peachtree City is a small master-planned community of about thirty-five thousand. It's known for its ninety miles of golf cart paths that network among pine tree-lined paths and under bridges. Peachtree City is south of Atlanta and lies between the city of Senoia, home of *The Walking Dead* television production, and Fayetteville, home of Pinewood Film Studios. Pinewood numbers eighteen sound stages and is bristling with major film production, including Marvel Studios blockbuster movies. I bought a home in Village Park, a planned over-fifty-five development, made new friends, and live in a friendly community where neighbors look out for one another. The motto is "Need anything, just ask."

With family

Chapter 59

News Now

Today, Columbia Square at 6121 Sunset Boulevard (the corner of Sunset and Gower) is no more. The historic building constructed in 1938 was home to radio, television, and Columbia Records for many years. It was designated a historic cultural monument in 2009 by the Los Angeles Cultural Heritage Commission and the Los Angeles city council. Today, a new building, NeueHouse, made up of residential and office space, stands in the former Columbia Square location. NeueHouse preserved some of the history of the square. An upscale restaurant, Paley's, is located at the Sunset and Gower corner, space that was at one time the Bank of America, followed by Channel 2's newsroom. The newsroom was later relocated to the west side of Columbia Square when Columbia Records moved out of the building; it remained at that location for many years. Channel 2, KCBS News is currently located at the Studio City lot in the San Fernando Valley.

As for my life and news today, I still get an adrenaline rush when there is a breaking news story. Staying abreast of current news events keeps the brain active. My doctor agrees. I'm retired; however, I've never lost the curiosity and passion I had when working in news all those years. You can take the woman out of the newsroom, but you can't take the newsroom out of the woman.

Acknowledgments

Many thanks to my family and friends for their continued support and love during the writing of this book. Thanks to my former colleagues in news who encouraged me to write about the good times and the bad at Channel 2 News in Los Angeles. We are, and will remain, a family who held together through numerous news director and general manager changes. Thanks for a lifetime of friendship.

Thanks to CBS Alumni for providing the CBS Columbia Square and CBS Television City photos. Thanks to Tom Ross for assisting with photo reproductions for this book.

Special thanks to my granddaughter, Kim Antell, for her love and support throughout my writing and for her role as editor of *Lifetime of News*.

·

About the Author

Lorraine Hillman is an award-winning news journalist, who worked for thirty-eight years at CBS, KCBS-TV (formerly KNXT) Channel 2 News, followed by two years at the ABC News bureau in Los Angeles. She is the recipient of two Emmy awards; eight Golden Mikes from the Radio and Television News Association; an Ohio State award for excellence; Los Angeles Press Club awards; and a Sigma Delta Chi journalism award.

Golden Mikes were awarded in 1990 for coverage of the McMartin verdict(McMartin began in 1983. A call to the Manhattan Beach Police Department from Judy Johnson asserting her son had been molested at the McMartin school day care. What followed was a frenzy of allegations, many bizarre, a six year trial, nationwide stories, unsubstantiated and a witch hunt of other day care centers. Channel 2 was slow on picking up on the McMartin story; it had been reported by Channel 7's Wayne Satz for several days. There were accusations of teachers taking children on plane rides to secret locations and underground tunnels. Our news director called the staff together and issued an ultimatum that we must catch up with Channel 7; pressure was on to lead with a McMartin story each day. I researched background on key figures, family members and teachers at the pre-school. Six years of trials, costing $15 million, and at the end no convictions.) and again in 1990 for "Stunt Deaths" with correspondent Lucrezia Cuen. Three Golden Mikes were awarded for earthquake coverage: in 1987 for "Earthquake: Preparing for the Big One"; in 1991 for breaking news coverage of the Sierra Madre Quake; and in 1994 for best continuing coverage of the Northridge Earthquake. Additionally, in 1992, she was the recipient of a Golden Mike merit award from the Radio and Television News Association of Southern California for best continuing coverage of the Los Angeles riot.

She received an Emmy Award in 1992 with correspondent Bob Jimenez and editor Allan Pena for "Anatomy of a Riot," coverage of the Los Angeles riot.

Mayor Tom Bradley of Los Angeles and the Los Angeles city council recognized her career in television news when she was presented a proclamation on February 9, 1995. The Los Angeles County Board of Supervisors presented a proclamation honoring her long career in Los Angeles television, starting with her earlier career during live programming at CBS Television City and followed by her nearly four decades in television news at Los Angeles Station KCBS, Channel 2.

She is a member of the Academy of Television Arts and Sciences; CBS Alumni, made up of retired CBS employees..and Pacific Pioneers, an organization recognizing the accomplishments of those in radio, television, and motion pictures.

Los Angeles Mayor Tom Bradley honoring my lifetime in News

Emmy Awards with Al Pena and Bob Jimenez

Emmy Awards, L to R, Pete Noyes, Larry Perret,
myself, Bill Applegate and Jay Strong